20TH-CENTURY COMPOSERS

Anton von Webern

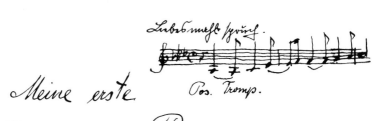

Meine erste

Bayreuther Reise.

August 1902.

Nach schlaflos verbrachter Nacht fuhr ich Dienstag
den 29. ~~August~~ Juli 1902. vom Berghof am
Schloss Hof um mit Tobst zusammen zu kommen.
Von hier bezw. Glandorf fuhren wir um
Mitternacht weg nach Salzburg, von hier durch
herrliche Salzkammergut bis Altmünster.
Das Salzkammergut ist reizend. Herrlich liegt
der Hallstädter See, mit dem gleichnamigen Ort
dessen weiße Giebelhäuser mit den grünen
Fenster leider immer ungemein lieblichen
Anblick bieten. Auch der Ebensee mit den
Menschen ~~der~~ gewährt dem Auge köstlichen
Reiz. --- Von Altmünster ging die Fahrt
weiter über Ried, Schärding nach Passau.
In Passau betraten wir bayerischen Boden.
♂ Herrliches Bayern! ~~Das~~ gibt's noch Leben.

Anton von Webern

by Malcolm Hayes

Φ

Phaidon Press Limited
Regent's Wharf
All Saints Street
London N1 9PA

First published 1995
© 1995 Phaidon Press Limited

ISBN 0 7148 3157 3

A CIP catalogue record for this book is
available from the British Library

Printed in Singapore

Frontispiece, a page from
Webern's diary recording
his pilgrimage to the
Wagner festival at Bayreuth
in 1902, and quoting the
'love feast' motif
(*Liebesmahl-Spruch*) from
Wagner's opera *Parsifal*
which Webern heard there.

Contents

Preface

Anyone writing a biography of Webern at the present time is in the unusual situation of having only one major published source of documentation on which to draw. I therefore wish to record a significant debt to Hans Moldenhauer's *Anton von Webern: A Chronicle of his Life and Work* (New York, Alfred A. Knopf Inc., and London, Victor Gollancz Ltd) regarding information on the facts of Webern's life. The humanity and the prodigious scholarship of Dr Moldenhauer's monumental chronicle, written in collaboration with his wife Rosaleen Moldenhauer, are warmly recommended to anyone wishing to explore Webern's life, work and world in closer detail.

Meanwhile it should go without saying that all views expressed, interpretations suggested, or conclusions drawn in the present study concerning any aspect of Webern's life and work, or any other topic, are entirely my own. I wish to make this very clear.

The extracts from Webern's letters to Hildegard Jone and Josef Humplik, and from Hildegard Jone's tribute to Webern on his fiftieth birthday, are taken from the English translation by Cornelius Cardew of Anton Webern: *Letters to Hildegard Jone and Josef Humplik*, edited by Josef Polnauer and published by Theodore Presser Company, Pennsylvania, in association with Universal Edition, London and Vienna. (Hildegard Jone's tribute was originally published in February 1934 in the Viennese periodical *23*, edited by Willi Reich.) The extracts from Webern's lecture series *The Path to the New Music* (edited by Willi Reich) are taken from the English translation by Leo Black, published also by Theodore Presser (copyright since assigned to Universal Edition Publishing Inc., New Jersey, USA). Those from Luigi Dallapiccola's 'Pages from a Diary' are taken from *Tempo* No. 99 (Boosey and Hawkes Music Publishers Ltd, 1972); the translation is by John C. G. Waterhouse. Quotations by Eduard Steuermann are taken from *The Not Quite Innocent Bystander*, a collection of writings edited by Clara Steuermann, David Porter, and Gunther Schuller, translated by Richard Cantwell and Charles Messner, and published by the University of Nebraska Press.

Extracts from Webern's letters to Schoenberg, from his diaries, notebooks, and sketchbooks, and from Hildegard Jone's poem beginning 'The sunlight speaks' (from her *Lumen* cycle) are taken from Hans Moldenhauer's *Anton von Webern: A Chronicle of his Life and Work.* I have also followed Hans and Rosaleen Moldenhauer's translations of material originally in German (except as indicated above), including reviews and reports taken from German and Austrian newspapers and periodicals of the time. My principal (though far from exclusive) historical source has been Barbara Jelavich's indispensable *Modern Austria: Empire and Republic, 1815–1986* (Cambridge University Press).

Nomenclature presents a few problems which necessitate consistency within a broader, perhaps illogical inconsistency. Until 1933, when he moved to the USA, Arnold Schoenberg was of course Arnold Schönberg; however the anglicized version of his surname is now so widely accepted in the German-speaking world as elsewhere that I have here used it throughout. Josef Hueber likewise replaces Josef Hüber. But I have resisted the anglicized use of first names; the Polish-born Eduard Steuermann, for instance, supplants the Edward Steuermann who lived in the USA from 1936 onwards.

Even the name of the book's subject gives scope for ambiguity. The constitution of the First Austrian Republic in 1920 officially abolished the trappings of aristocratic nomenclature such as the 'von' in, for instance, Anton von Webern. Its use never entirely disappeared, however, and since the birth of the Second Republic in 1945 it has been widely restored. Rather than attempt to edit in (or out) the 'von' attaching to Webern's name at any or every point, I have simply retained whichever version appears in the original source. This applies also to the titles of articles and books on Webern listed in the bibliography at the end of this volume.

A book may be written in isolation, but the ideas that nurture it come from many sources, often personal ones. Above all I would like to offer the warmest of thanks to Peter and Hedi Stadlen for sharing with me their reminiscences of Webern himself, and of day-to-day life in Austria between the two World Wars. Special thanks are also extended to Norman Lebrecht for originally suggesting the idea of this book; for his unquenchable encouragement while it was being written; and for the loan of some source material which I suspect I would otherwise have overlooked.

Among a constellation of friends, Bernard Benoliel, David Stevens and Andrew Stewart each participated in a sequence of lively conversations on various aspects of Webern's life and work. My mother and father offered their usual generous hospitality, during a visit to their home in the north of Scotland, whenever I came up for air between long sessions of researching the history of the Austro-Hungarian Empire. Dr Felix Meyer, curator of the Webern Archive in the Paul Sacher Foundation in Basel, helpfully supplied information on Webern's orchestral arrangement of Martin Plüddemann's ballad *Siegfrieds Schwert*. Jeremy Upton of the Reid Library in Edinburgh University's Music Department kindly arranged for a former student to peruse Webern's doctoral thesis on Heinrich Isaac in *Denkmäler der Tonkunst in Österreich*.

The team at Phaidon Press deserve my limitless gratitude for their patience as the completion of this book sailed ever further past the agreed deadline. Last and far from least I would like to thank the people of Austria, and of Klagenfurt and Semmering in particular, for the kindness and courtesy which have made my visits to their country in connection with the book a happy memory in their own right.

Malcolm Hayes
London, 1995

Opposite, a typical scene in Carinthia in southern Austria: Millstatt on the Millstätter See, viewed westwards towards the town of Seeboden in the distance.

Prelude

This is not a polemical book. During the past half-century
Webern's work has had such an assortment of critical, ideological,
and analytical Taj Mahals constructed around it – most of them
conspicuously lacking the elegance of the original building – that
many potential listeners have by now been put off approaching his
music at all. This biography has therefore been written with a very
different purpose in mind. I hope it may help a little to dismantle
some of the soulless intellectual barriers which, for far too long, have
been allowed to come between new listeners and the work of this
admittedly uncompromising, but far from truly 'difficult' composer.

For most non-specialist music-lovers – as for plenty of specialist
ones – Webern's music does often seem difficult in the sense that it
does not sound like Tchaikovsky's or Mozart's. Meanwhile I am sure
that anyone curious enough to have opened a book on Webern and
to have read this far down the page will be prepared to start from
the position that his music, like anyone else's, is in the business of
sounding like itself. Its tendency to extreme concentration and brevity
can seem bewildering at first, but in most other respects Webern is
in fact a rather less difficult composer than many other leading lights
of the twentieth century. He is not concerned to dazzle, seduce, or
flatter to deceive; each of his ultra-compressed works sets out its store
with exceptional clarity and honesty. You always know where you
stand with Webern. And he never wastes your time.

Much of what has been written about his music gives the
impression that it is (a) modern, (b) theoretical, (c) abstract, and (d)
formidably complicated. In one sense it could be argued that all these
descriptions (not necessarily derogatory in themselves) are true and,
in another, that none of them is. Abstract musical thought did
matter to Webern; for him, notes or groups of notes played grave
and beautiful games with each other just as, for the ancient Greeks,
numbers and symbols did. In the natural world – which for him
meant the Austrian mountains, their plants and flowers, and their

lake-studded foothills – he similarly discerned an underlying unity of all creation, and his later work especially is a musical represent-ation of this vision of the heart of things. He had a deep interest in art-forms other than his own, and while it is unlikely that the post-impressionist style of the French painter Paul Cézanne could have been to his personal taste, he might well have sensed an affinity with Cézanne's stated intention to depict the sun-burnished, breeze-swept landscapes of Provence in terms of three basic units of construction, 'the cone, the sphere, and the cylinder'. In the same way, Webern's idea of the art of composing drove him on a lifelong and obsessive quest to find, beyond the surface beauty of musical expression, a way of articulating the deeper beauty of the bone-structure beneath.

But this preoccupation with autonomous sound-structures was only one aspect of his art. Webern was also an instinctively vocal composer whose love of opera, choral music, and song dominated both his life and his work in various ways. An innate and spontan-eous lyricism operates in his music at every level, from its sharply individual sense of proportion and phrasing down to the impulse linking each single note to the next, as heartbeat follows heartbeat.

He was a radical composer in both senses of the word, gifted with a fanatically exploratory musical mind which was also profoundly and proudly rooted in the heritage of the past. His legacy is an output which bestrides both the powerful inheritance of the nineteenth-century Austro-German musical tradition, and the ensuing era of twentieth-century modernism which his own work did much to initiate and (posthumously) develop. His life-story similarly brims with apparent contradictions. While the course of his professional musical career was often confused and sometimes shambolic, his sense of his artistic direction as a composer was unshakeably sure from an early age. He lived and worked almost all his life in or near big cities (as most working musicians have to), yet was perhaps only truly at peace with himself when walking or climbing among the high peaks of the Austrian Alps. During both World Wars he attached himself without inhibition to the pan-German militaristic bandwagon of the times; in the intervening years he lived a life that was a model of peaceable, family-orientated domesticity. From the mid-1930s onwards he continued to support Nazi rule in Austria and Germany even when those same rulers had banned performances of his own music on the grounds that it was 'degenerate'. His pro-Nazi stance at this time alienated many of those close to him; at the same time he repeatedly helped and supported Jewish friends and colleagues, sometimes at serious risk to himself. A fluent and prolific composer when young, during the last seventeen years of his life he completed just ten works, none of them over fifteen minutes long.

It is of course debatable as to how far a biographical study can convey anything essential about a composer's music beyond what the reader can absorb simply by listening to it (which is what counts). But a biography can at least widen the perspective by exploring the world in which that composer lived and worked, and where his music in that sense came from. Outwardly, Webern's story is also Austria's story. His life and personality encapsulate the social and political ambiguities (some of them unsavoury) first of the waning Austro-Hungarian Empire, then of the troubled, newly founded Austrian nation-state in the first half of the twentieth century. Meanwhile his inner, artistic life was broadly self-sufficient from the start and became increasingly so as the years passed, following a path ever more detached and solitary – as climbing a mountain is a journey from idyllic wooded foothills, by way of spacious upland pastures, towards an isolated rocky peak.

Above all, Webern represents an extreme case of an artist on whom all the crucial influences were early ones. So this is where his story must start.

I

A portrait photograph of Webern
taken in Stettin, 1912

Only when a life, an art, is restricted to the
most important things, only then can they
unfold to their fullest richness … In a letter to
me Anton Webern wrote the following very
beautiful sentence: 'Through my work, all that
is past becomes like a childhood.' Where this
lovely process of friendly humanity occurs in an
art, there is really no room for the slightest trace
of anything that does not belong.

Hildegard Jone, on the occasion of
Webern's fiftieth birthday, December 1933

Beginnings 1883-1904

Almost every region of Austria is beautiful to look at; the countryside around Klagenfurt in Carinthia is more beautiful than most. The best way to approach it is from the north, along one of several routes that wind through the clustered pinnacles and spires of the Salzburg Alps and across the Hohe Tauern range which forms the backbone of modern Austria. Spread out along the southern flank of the Hohe Tauern is the province of Carinthia, a narrow strip of territory some 150 kilometres long, 50 kilometres wide from north to south, and stretching from East Tyrol and Italy in the west to Styria and Slovenia in the east.

As one comes down from the central mountains, a landscape unfolds which is quite different from the picture-postcard spectacle of the Alps on their northern side. Klagenfurt, Carinthia's main town, is idyllically situated at the eastern end of the Wörthersee, at the centre of a plain, ringed in the middle distance by mountains whose peaks and ridges gently punctuate the skyline. The valleys that lead away eastwards towards the central European plain are wider, gentler, and less obviously dramatic than those to the north.

Carinthia's main town, Klagenfurt, viewed eastwards from the Wörthersee; a part of the country in which Anton von Webern grew up

Klagenfurt am Wörthersee

The colours, too, are different: the weather systems that sweep in from the Atlantic Ocean and northern Europe drop most of their rain on the mountains to the west, so that the Carinthian countryside has a drier, leaner look than the lush greenness of the Bavarian and Tyrolean foothills. Rich, undulating farmland rolls from horizon to horizon, its fertility tempered by the gentle austerity of fir and pine. It is a benign landscape, almost consciously seeming to rein in any sense of self-display; the villages that here dot the hills and valleys lack the element of picturesque self-advertisement from which their Salzburg and Tyrolean counterparts, appealing to the eye as they are, seldom seem entirely immune. Even the tree-shrouded Carinthian hills emanate a quiet, knowing permanence that haunts the mind just as deeply as does the grandeur of the towering peaks away to the north and west. This is the country where Anton von Webern grew up.

His ancestry has been traced back as far as the fifteenth century, when a family originating from Bohemia in the present-day Czech Republic, and bearing the more usual German name of Weber, settled in what is now South Tyrol in Italy. Two brothers were elevated to the nobility by the Habsburg Emperor Maximilian II, and in the early eighteenth century a subsequent decree confirming the family's noble rank refers to their name as 'von Webern'. The first of Anton von Webern's forebears known to have moved to the more low-lying country to the east was his great-grandfather, Josef Eduard von Webern, who married in Marburg on the river Drau (now Maribor on the river Drava in Slovenia) and set himself up as a liqueur manufacturer, before taking up the less exotic profession of tax assessor in the town of Pettau. Josef Eduard's eldest son, Anton, became a mining engineer based in Liescha, where in 1846 he married the daughter of a prominent family of local landowners. Through his wife, this earlier Anton duly inherited the 500-acre estate of Preglhof near the village of Schwabegg in Lower Carinthia, some forty kilometres east of Klagenfurt.

The oldest of Anton senior's five children, Carl, followed in his father's professional footsteps; after school at the Klagenfurt Gymnasium, and legal and political studies at Graz and Vienna Universities, he too qualified as a mining engineer following studies at the School of Mining in Leoben in the province of Styria. While there he met Amalie Geer, the daughter of a local landlord and master

Above, Carl von Webern, the composer's father; *right,* Webern's mother with her three children (left to right): Rosa, Anton and Maria in the 1880s

butcher, and married her in 1877 despite temporary resistance from his own family on the grounds of his bride's inferior social status. Carl von Webern's professional expertise soon marked him out as a high-flyer, and after a period of army service (during which he was decorated for bravery in combat, in Bosnia-Hercegovina in 1881) he embarked on a civil service career which necessitated a peripatetic existence for him and his young family. A few years in Olmütz were followed by a period in Vienna, where Carl von Webern served in the Ministry of Agriculture of the Austrian government. It was in Vienna that Amalie gave birth to the fourth of their five children, of which two, a son and a daughter, had already died in infancy. So Anton Friedrich Wilhelm, born on 3 December 1883 at Löwengasse 53a in the third district of Vienna, was to be their only surviving son.

In 1889 Carl von Webern was promoted to the post of Councillor of Mining and was transferred to Graz, the capital city of Styria. In 1894 the family moved once again – to Klagenfurt, where Webern's father, again promoted, was made Chief Councillor of Mining, a post he was to hold there for the next eight years. Young Anton was therefore fortunate to find himself growing up in two towns notable

Opposite, the Herrengasse in the centre of Klagenfurt, the town in which Webern spent his formative years

for their exquisite settings. Graz, which is itself a formidably handsome town compared to the more genial and homespun Klagenfurt,
is no less attractively situated in the spacious Styrian countryside,
with mountain peaks rising evocatively in the far distance. Webern's
primary schooling continued in Graz until he was eleven, when his
father's transfer to Klagenfurt necessitated his enrolment in the town's
Gymnasium school.

Webern's academic record in the years that followed was that of
an average student: reasonably conscientious and, like most
schoolchildren, better at some subjects than at others. It is worth
remarking that this composer-to-be of supposedly 'mathematical'
music (as posthumous legend would have it) in fact showed almost
no aptitude for mathematics and physics throughout his school
career. Music, however, was also a part of the Gymnasium syllabus,
and here Webern did consistently well – no surprise in one whose
unusual gifts in this direction had already long been evident.

His father was not particularly musical. Webern seems to have
inherited his talent almost entirely from his mother, who besides
being a good pianist was also – to judge from the recorded memories
of his younger sister Rosa – an accomplished singer. Webern had
adored his mother from an early age, and the musical bond between
them was further to deepen his devotion to her in the years to come.
It was Amalie von Webern who gave her son his first proper piano
lessons at the age of five, by which time he had already learned to
sing along accurately to his mother's playing. He himself soon began
to develop into a competent pianist, taking up the cello as well when
the family moved to Klagenfurt. Webern's older sister, Maria, was
also a pianist, and Rosa played the violin, so that the three
children were able to play trios together, along with original works
and arrangements for their individual solo instruments with
piano accompaniment.

Klagenfurt at this time offered a level of cultural and musical
activity much livelier and more extensive than its provincial status
might indicate. This was not an unusual situation in German-
speaking communities, where an interest in playing classical music
was considered a normal part of life in civilized human society,
rather than one of the trappings of up-market status (an attitude
typical of the enlightened cultural values which persist to this day).

Opera and concert performances took place regularly, with local talent often to the fore. In 1898 a proud fourteen-year-old by the name of Anton von Webern was accepted into the cello section of the orchestra of Klagenfurt's Konzertverein (concert society), and in this way began to gain his first inside experience of the symphonic repertory.

But most of all, and like most schoolchildren, Webern lived for his holidays. As the eldest son of Anton von Webern senior, Carl von Webern had inherited the Preglhof estate on his father's death in 1889. Every spring and summer the family would leave Klagenfurt and head for their ancestral home in the Lower Carinthian countryside. It is fitting that one of the two earliest musical works by Webern to have survived – a pair of untitled pieces for cello and piano – is dated 'Preglhof, 17 September 1899'.

To suggest that the house and its surrounding landscape held a central place in Webern's heart merely as the location of idyllic

The Webern family at the Preglhof, 17 May 1887. At the centre is Anton von Webern senior, the composer's grandfather. Young Anton's father and mother are at the upper and lower right of the group. Webern's cousin Ernst Diez is second from left in the front row; Webern himself is seated at his grandfather's feet.

The Preglhof, Webern's
ancestral home, c.1900

summer holidays would be to underestimate the power of the near-
untranslatable concept of *Heimat* over the Austro-German soul.
Literally 'homeland', the word is also replete with related allusions
that resonate within a much wider and deeper psychological
perspective than mere geographical recollection. One's *Heimat* is,
besides these things, the essential spiritual well-spring of one's life: the
source which, down the years to come, continues to cradle, nurture,
and sustain one's being. Whether or not you respond to its pull by
actually returning to live there in later life – or by never leaving in the
first place – is, in the deepest sense, immaterial; spiritually, the die has
been cast. The Preglhof and its surrounding hills and farmland were
Webern's *Heimat*.

The house itself is an ample, three-storeyed building nestling at
the foot of a tree-covered hill rising to the south; sited adjacent to it
at right angles, as if by a designer's unerring eye, is a long, brick-built
barn of the kind typical of the region. The Preglhof and its outlying
buildings are perched on a gentle rise in the ground, so that they
command a full and spacious view of the wide, flat stretch of
farmland to the north. The river Drau flows broadly past, eastwards
in the direction of Slovenia; beyond it, the next range of hills rises to
the skyline. In the middle distance, on a promontory bounded by a
bend in the river, the village of Schwabegg lies at the heart of its

surrounding fields. The spires of its two churches are visible for miles around.

A landscape like this – not just generally flat, but level as a millpond – seems to emanate a particular kind of quietness and peace. Meanwhile the sense of Schwabegg's vast surrounding spaces is rendered at once less oppressive and more vivid by the outline of the low Carinthian hills rising in the distance. Childhood memories have a way of retaining and constantly reinventing their haunting sharpness of focus down the years. Anyone wondering at the extent to which the triple themes of landscape, nature, and the mountains were to obsess Webern throughout his life need only set eyes on Schwabegg and its setting – as if a slice of remotest Lincolnshire had been dropped down among the foothills of the Alps – for whole worlds within his music, hitherto perhaps only half-sensed, to become unforgettably clear. The unique atmosphere of Webern's later works, whose concentration of utterance seems suspended within a surrounding stillness at once intense and benign, relates back unmistakably to the Preglhof, the dream-like loveliness of its position, and the fields of Carinthia stretching away into the distance.

The house's position is strange in one respect: it is tucked in so close to the north-facing hill behind it that it could almost have been designed to catch the minimum of sunlight. But there was nothing sunless about Webern's upbringing there. His love of the outdoors, counterbalancing the intellectual and artistic flair that he showed from an early age, was firmly implanted by those early summers at the Preglhof. Life on the land in that part of Europe, while still largely feudal in structure, was not as rigidly class-demarcated as it was in England, and there is nothing surprising in Rosa von Webern's recollection that her brother loved to join in the work at harvest time. She also recounts an amusing anecdote which shows that already, in life as in his work, it was not in Webern's nature to do things by halves. One summer, when he was seventeen, a fire raged through the estate's farmland, destroying that season's crop and threatening the house itself. The fire brigade from the town of Bleiburg, a few miles away to the south, failed to arrive in time, and all local hands were summoned to the rescue. According to Rosa, her brother 'assisted very vigorously in this, pouring water from a bucket onto the manor house. The fire excited him so much that for many nights afterwards

Following page, Schwabegg, part of Webern's Heimat, as it appears today viewed from the south. The River Drau flows eastwards between the village and the hills in the background.

he got up in his sleep and doused the walls of his room with water from the pitcher.'

His studies in Klagenfurt had developed by this time to a point where it was clear to Webern himself, if not to his parents, that music was to be his life. Every young musician, however talented, needs to be lucky enough also to find good teachers. Webern was fortunate from the age of fourteen onwards to be taken under the wing of Edwin Komauer, a financial official in Klagenfurt whose daily duties, in the time-honoured manner of imperial bureaucracies, did not require him to remain at the office any later than two o'clock in the afternoon. Komauer was therefore free to place his excellent musical skills at the service of the town's cultural life, and duly did so – playing the piano, accompanying, conducting, teaching, and composing. His new young pupil now found his busy schedule at the Gymnasium supplemented by an extra-curricular course of study which was to lay an ideal foundation for the years of creative struggle to come.

Komauer was instinctively responsive to the trends of the new music of the day, whose leading lights were Richard Wagner (who had died only recently, in the year of Webern's birth) and Richard Strauss. These two figures, whose work is now ranked among the central pillars of the Austro-German repertory, were then considered violently controversial. Musical circles in the German-speaking world were split into two camps, polarized around the explicit creative radicalism of Wagner – who in his music-dramas such as *Tristan und Isolde*, *Parsifal*, and his four-part 'Ring' cycle had specifically set out to revolutionize opera as an art-form – and the implicit conservatism of Johannes Brahms, who composed no opera and concentrated instead on symphonies, concertos, and chamber music. Later generations, able to view the controversy in a longer perspective, have more accurately perceived the truth of the situation: that Wagner's achievement was one of renewal and development rather than of iconoclasm, and that Brahms, too, had been extending the scope of the symphony in the post-Beethoven age with results more radical than his music's relatively traditional tone suggests.

But this was not how the issue was seen at the time, and debate on the subject was no doubt as partisan in the concert-halls and living rooms of Klagenfurt as it was elsewhere. Richard Strauss's early symphonic poems had subsequently exploded onto a startled German concert scene with the impact that Wagner had already made on opera. Strauss – no relation, incidentally, to the waltz- and polka-composing Strauss dynasty of Vienna – was later to consolidate his position as one of the major musical figures of his generation with a long sequence of operas (*Der Rosenkavalier* pre-eminent among them) whose relationship to tradition, though subtle, is direct. But when Webern was young, Strauss was perceived as the iconoclastic firebrand of the age, who was transferring the new and disturbing chromatic expressiveness of Wagnerian opera to the concert-hall. Another important example for Webern was the Austrian composer Hugo Wolf, the main part of whose output consists almost entirely of songs for voice and piano – songs which remarkably fuse the new Wagnerian intensity of style and harmony with the song-writing tradition developed earlier in the century by Franz Schubert and Robert Schumann. Wolf's music, which favoured the intimate Lied rather than the grander public forum of the orchestral concert-hall, was less famous than Strauss's, but it was already known in informed musical circles.

Komauer was a teacher with musical values broad enough to encompass all these various trends. An enthusiastic Wagnerian, he also believed in giving his pupils a solid grounding in traditional musical theory and technique, and the young Webern was duly put through a thorough course of study of the work of an earlier German musical giant, Johann Sebastian Bach. The greatness of Bach's achievement relates to the age in which he lived: a century and a half before that of Wagner and Brahms, and informed by a quite different set of values. Wagner epitomized the nineteenth-century age of Romanticism and its idea of the artist as attention-seeking hero. In Bach's time, however, music was still perceived primarily in terms of its functional contribution to existing institutions of human activity – the church, the theatre, the court – rather than as a soul-nourishing component of the leisure-time of an educated urban middle class. A musical work spoke spiritually, as a self-contained, perfectly functioning artefact, rather than emotionally, as a 'work of art'. (This may have been what Bach meant when he was quoted as saying that in musical composition there was no such thing as inspiration, only hard work.)

It was Bach's achievement to fuse this traditional, functionally based perception of music's purpose with the new expressive possibilities offered by the growing technical advances of instrumental performance. The greatness of his finest work is that it achieves this artistic balance without compromising either aspect. Two centuries later, with the style and sound-world of Western music now utterly transformed, the example of Bach's method was nonetheless to remain of great importance to Webern. One wonders, however, how the pedagogically inclined Komauer would have reacted if he had been able to foresee the explosive creative direction in which, within just a few years, his teaching of this talented young pupil was to lead.

It is not known for certain exactly how early in his childhood Webern began to compose. No juvenilia from a very early age survive, although that is not in itself reason to assume that he did not try his hand at composing as a small boy. Apart from the two simple pieces for cello and piano already mentioned, all the music he is known to

Webern's early composer-heroes included Wagner, *left*, and Hugo Wolf (photographed in 1895), *right*.

have composed in his youthful Klagenfurt years consists of songs for voice and piano. Eight have survived which were written before the family moved to Vienna in 1902 though, since these were only discovered some years after Webern's death, it is possible that other songs or purely instrumental pieces may yet come to light. If Webern was indeed concentrating exclusively on composing songs at this time, then an accurate indication is given of how his musical preferences were subsequently to develop. In the light of his posthumous deification in the 1950s by the European avant garde as the creator of purely abstract works, it cannot be stressed too strongly that Webern was first and foremost a vocal composer. In every phase of his output – even in the sequence of late masterpieces which became a collective totem for that same avant garde – Webern's vocal works outnumber his purely instrumental ones. In the early 1950s, when much of his music was still unpublished and some of his major works had not yet even been performed, there was arguably some excuse for the misrepresentation of this central aspect of his life's work. In the present age there is none whatever. From the start, composing for the voice was Webern's deepest instinct as a composer. It was to remain so always.

His mother's singing voice must have been a natural encouragement for this burgeoning interest. So was Webern's own appetite for literature. Like many an artistically smitten youngster he read voraciously from an early age, and his choice of texts in his songs reflects his affinity with the lyric poets of his own and earlier generations: Ferdinand Avenarius, Richard Dehmel, Theodor Storm, Goethe. Fired with enthusiasm, Webern tried his hand at writing his own poems in a similar style. He copied these into one of the series of diaries and notebooks he had begun to fill with whatever captured his interest. Poems, extracts from novels and philosophical works, articles on music, impressions of concerts in Klagenfurt would here be written down with the meticulous care for detail that was to remain typical of every aspect of his work in the years to come.

Webern's first known song-setting is of the poem *Vorfrühling* ('Early Spring') by Avenarius; the earliest of its several manuscript copies, doubtless made with local performances in mind, is dated 'Klagenfurt, 1899'. Care must be taken when trying to trace affinities, however conveniently clear they may seem, between a composer's mature work and a single song written when he may have been no more than fifteen years old. Webern's style was soon to develop so rapidly that it can be difficult for the ear to sense any connection between the startlingly modernist stance of his music written from about 1909 onwards and a work like *Vorfrühling*, which dates from only ten years earlier. A glance at the manuscript of the song is enough to notice such similarities as the spare understatement of the writing, and the hypersensitive expression-markings with which Webern's later scores were to be obsessively studded: 'sehr leise' (very quiet), 'so zart als möglich' (as tenderly as possible), and so on.

What is much more striking to the ear, however, is *Vorfrühling*'s connection with Hugo Wolf's late-Romantic style of song-composing, and the remarkable extent to which the fifteen-year-old Webern had already absorbed Wolf's example. The poem itself suggests a musical approach of quiet restraint:

Softly enter –
No longer in deep sleep,
In light slumber only
Lies the countryside;
And the blackbird's early call
Already blends lovely morning images
Into his dream.

Webern's setting combines lyrical simplicity with a sonorous, drowsy pastoralism, achieving this with a minimum of effectively placed notes while avoiding anything so banal as an attempted imitation of the blackbird's song. Moreover this novice composer had already acquired the Wolfian art of presenting and working out a satisfyingly complete musical argument within the shortest of spaces. The music for the first four lines sets the tranquil scene; a hint of denser harmonic activity stirs in the next three; and a simple repeat of the first line and its accompaniment then rounds out the form with that quintessential song-composer's skill, a perfect sense of touch.

Webern's impressions of musical life in Klagenfurt at this time brim with the kind of opinionated enthusiasm characteristic of young people. A letter written to his cousin, Ernst Diez, in the autumn of 1900 is typical in its spirited and intemperate pen-portrait of an orchestral concert as observed from the vantage-point of the cello section.

Last Sunday we had a Musikverein concert, with a very tastelessly arranged programme: 'Elsa's Dream' from [Wagner's opera] Lohengrin, Mendelssohn's Violin Concerto and – now comes the idiocy – some songs, and then Beethoven's Ninth Symphony [the 'Choral'] with omission of the final movement for lack of chorus and soloists. The individual numbers are grand, but their juxtaposition is horrible. How can one sing, in so large a hall, songs with piano accompaniment before the Ninth! ... Of course, I played in the orchestra. But the indifference of people is stupendous. They must not have the slightest conception of what it means to perform Beethoven's Ninth ... The people simply go there, listen as if a salon polka was being played, and leave again without any sign of excitement. If everyone had felt what I as merely one of the players felt! ...

Diez was Webern's first cousin and best friend. The son of Carl von Webern's only sister Maria Luise and Friedrich Diez, Ernst was five years older than Webern; he was artistically inclined (later becoming an authority on Asian art), and shared his younger relative's love of music and the great outdoors. The Diez family lived in nearby Bleiburg, and Ernst regularly came to stay at the Preglhof in the school holidays, during which the two friends would devote many an hour to walking in the Schwabegg countryside and passionately discussing the great questions of Art, Life and Love. Webern liked the girls, and they appear to have liked him too, if a term-time letter to Diez in the autumn of 1900 is to be believed. Caught red-handed by some of the Gymnasium professors in a Klagenfurt coffee-house after a dancing lesson, Webern had been confined to barracks for the rest of the day and had been prevented from further pursuing this agreeable line of study. 'My mood is horrible,' he informed his cousin. 'You may not believe that I am so addicted to dancing, but – there is Stanzi [Constanza]! I am quite crazy about her. She is an enticing girl, full of temperament. Now I will probably see very little of her ... She is also rather well disposed towards me – right now this can be stated as a matter of fact.' He also voiced interest in one Frieda Hibler, suggesting to Diez that 'if you do not find Frieda too *schiach* [homely], I definitely advise you to take her, but you must leave

Gustav Mahler

The two great composer-
conductors of the German
and Austrian musical world
at the turn of the century:
Richard Strauss, *left,*
and Gustav Mahler, *right*

Stanzi for me'. Diez evidently took up the offer, to judge from the
letter Webern wrote to him on Frieda's behalf a year later; the
romance between her and Ernst had apparently terminated, and
Webern, acting as honourable go-between, asked Diez to return to
him her letters and photograph.

It was to Diez, too, that Webern conveyed his impressions of his
latest musical discoveries. In 1901 he first encountered the music
of Gustav Mahler, who had already emerged as the German musical
world's other towering contemporary figure besides Richard Strauss.
At this time the Austrian–Jewish Mahler was better known for
his meteoric rise as a conductor than for his own music. Four years
previously, at the age of only thirty-six, he had been appointed
Kapellmeister – effectively, musical and artistic director – of the
Vienna Court Opera (today the State Opera). Meanwhile his gigantic
symphonies, which combine fervent nature-worship and the
deliberate use of non-classical material – rustic dance-music, military

fanfares – with an unprecedentedly vivid psychological exploration of
the memories of Mahler's own fraught childhood, had as yet made
little headway with a bewildered musical public. Webern, however,
identified instantly and perceptively with Mahler's music. 'I liked it
very much,' he told Diez. 'Naturally, if one plays Richard Strauss
right after, or vice versa, one is bound to notice a great difference.
The themes of Strauss are much grander, more ingenious, more
powerful. Mahler's music makes an almost childlike impression,
despite the quite enormous orchestral apparatus.' At this time he also
heard a performance of Wagner's opera *Tristan und Isolde* in Graz, and
was overwhelmed. True to form he had done his homework,
and informed Diez that 'sitting in the first row of the parquet,
I could enjoy everything wonderfully, having thoroughly studied the
score beforehand, and thus I had an indescribable and unforget-
table experience'.

    Early in 1902 Webern's father was promoted to the Ministry of
Agriculture in Vienna. Instead of spending the Easter holiday at the
Preglhof as usual, the family decided to sample their new sur-

Wilhelmine Mörtl, Webern's
future wife, in 1901 at the age
of fifteen

roundings in the capital city of the Habsburg Empire. Webern promptly took himself along to the Court Opera to see *Götter-dämmerung*, the fourth and last opera of Wagner's 'Ring' cycle. The experience confirmed his Wagner-idolatry; he confided to himself in his diary that he 'trembled from emotion' as he played the music on the piano. Another fateful encounter of a different kind also took place at this time. Webern already knew his first cousin Wilhelmine Mörtl – the daughter of his mother's sister Maria and the Viennese notary Gustav Mörtl – but it seems they had not seen each other for some years. Wilhelmine was fifteen when she and Webern met again during that Easter in Vienna. The outcome was that the 'enticing' Stanzi and her peers in Klagenfurt no longer held any further interest for Webern. The attachment between the two cousins was to deepen from this point into an enduring and unshakeable love; there is no evidence that either of them, throughout the years to come, ever looked at anyone else.

With his family now living in Vienna, Webern spent his last term of study at the Klagenfurt Gymnasium as a boarder. As a reward for passing his final examinations, his father had promised him a trip to the Wagner festival held every summer in the Upper Franconian town of Bayreuth in Germany. Webern's four-day visit, made in company with Diez, was to remain for him one of the highlights of his life, and the evident intensity of his impressions may explain why – despite his undimmed admiration for Wagner's music in subsequent years – he never showed any inclination to return to Bayreuth and perhaps risk tarnishing this golden memory of his youth. He recorded the experience in his diary in exhaustive detail, including the exact timetable of the railway journey from Vienna to Bayreuth, his impressions of the route through the Salzkammergut region around Salzburg, of the festival theatre itself on the hill outside Bayreuth, and of the performances he heard there of Wagner's *Parsifal* – 'In the face of such magnificence, one can only sink to one's knees and pray in silent devotion' – and *Der fliegende Holländer* ('The Flying Dutchman').

Then as now, there was an opera-going element in the audience whose main purpose in making the annual pilgrimage to Bayreuth was to see and be seen, rather than to listen to the works of the Master with the reverence considered appropriate by the Wagner-

Ascent to the Festival Theatre, a painting by Otto von der Wehl, 1909, recording the atmosphere at Bayreuth which Webern visited in 1902

worshipping faithful. A fulminating diary entry leaves little doubt as to the camp with which Webern identified. 'This audience is as ill-mannered as that in a provincial town,' he fumed. 'It is revolting to see that people cannot keep quiet in the festival hall even after the music has begun, or while it still plays after the curtain has closed. Hardly has the crowd left the temple when laughing and idle chatter start again, when each one inspects the other's wardrobe and behaves as if he had not experienced at all something that transports our kind out of this world. And then! There was, on top of it, applause! If people start to applaud after the end of *Parsifal* it cannot be anything but a display of the greatest rudeness …'

'Our kind …' One must be careful not to read too much into a diary entry written by an impressionable and excited eighteen-year-old attending his first Bayreuth Festival. Wagner's music, after all, remains notorious for its capacity to polarize otherwise equable music-lovers into twin camps of preposterous idolatry on the one hand and near-apoplectic detestation on the other. But there is something ominous here in Webern's tone of fanatical censoriousness: the capacity for unbridled enthusiasm for his own point of view, combined with total and humourless intolerance of anyone who for any reason, trivial or otherwise, might think or behave differently.

On the journey home the two friends stopped off in Munich, where Diez was keen to fit in a visit to the city's art galleries. Webern, whose interest in fine art had already been stimulated by his cousin, was specially impressed by the work of the Italian–Swiss landscape painter Giovanni Segantini. Back home at the Preglhof, a day of reckoning approached concerning Webern's future. Understandably, his father had always wanted his only male heir to study agriculture, with a view eventually that he should inherit the Preglhof. This eminently reasonable scenario had since been complicated by Webern's implacable insistence that he wished 'to live only for Art'. Many a father of Carl von Webern's generation and social standing would have tried to bully his son into doing his bidding, but the distinguished mining official evidently and sensibly saw that this would be pointless. Accordingly a patriarchal conclave of musically knowledgeable friends of the family assembled at the Preglhof to preside over a kind of informal examination of the young musician, who was required to play one of his own compositions besides demonstrating his performing skills. (Webern later confided to Diez that he had carefully selected one of his least far-out and potentially upsetting creations for the occasion.) The consensus was that young Anton was indeed made of the right stuff to persevere along the stony path of a professional musical career. Carl von Webern insisted, however, that his son's further education should be more broadly based than would be possible at a musical conservatoire. So, in the autumn of 1902, Webern enrolled at the University of Vienna to study musical history in conjunction with lecture courses in philosophy, literature and fine art.

Though he cannot have known it, his life had already reached a watershed. Newly arrived as a student in the spectacular capital city of the Austrian Empire, brimming with enthusiasm for his new studies, and finding himself living in the same town as Wilhelmine Mörtl, Webern must have felt that the happiest part of his life was just beginning. But in a deeper sense it had already ended. From now on the idyll of those early Preglhof years was gradually to become ever more remote. The nature of turn-of-the-century life in the Habsburg capital – outwardly unquenchably hedonistic, inwardly fraught with instability, unease and incipient racial prejudice – meant that Webern now found himself living in a political, social and cultural cauldron that before long was to boil over. The next fifty years were to encompass one of the most turbulent periods, both in peace and in war, in Viennese history. The root causes of that turbulence reached far back through the centuries.

The imperial world into which Webern was born is indicated only deceptively by the outline of modern Austria on the map of Europe. Carinthia, for instance, now lies at the south of the small, landlocked, almost exclusively German-speaking territory whose borders were demarcated by the victorious powers, at the end of the First World War in 1918, as the Republic of Austria. Webern grew up in an empire whose ethnic and political make-up was much more confused and complex. Austria–Hungary, as it was clumsily known, represented the last intact enclave of the Habsburg Empire, which in the mid-sixteenth century had encompassed almost half of Europe. And

Designs by Koloman Moser for postage stamps celebrating the diamond jubilee of the reign of Franz Joseph I, 1908

Franz Joseph I, Habsburg Emperor from 1848 to 1916

Carinthia, far from being a southern outpost of a modern nation state, was one of the most westerly provinces of an elaborate assembly of German-, Hungarian-, Czech-, and Polish-speaking regions.

The Habsburg Empire – the name derives from the ancestral residence of its first rulers, Habichtsburg or 'Hawk's Castle' in Switzerland – first crystallized around the German-speaking territories of what are now Vienna, Upper Austria, and Lower Austria in the early fourteenth century. Within 200 years an elaborate series of alliances, military campaigns, and royal marriages had created a vast empire that included Spain, the recent Spanish conquests in newly discovered America, Sardinia, Sicily, more than half of Italy, the Netherlands, Burgundy, and several of the German-speaking states to the north of the Austrian lands – to say nothing of a swathe of immediately adjacent territory stretching unbroken from Vorarlberg on the Swiss border in the west to Transylvania in the east (almost as far as the Black Sea), and from Bohemia and Silesia in the north to the Dalmatian coast on the Adriatic in the south. The awareness that such a diverse and far-flung empire had effectively become ungovernable as a single unit led to its division in the mid-sixteenth century; the western half was then ruled from Spain, while at the heart of the eastern territories were Vienna and the adjacent Austrian Hereditary Lands. (The German name for Austria, Österreich, translates as 'eastern empire'.)

The next three and a half centuries were to witness a period of gradual but relentless decline, as the political and administrative unity ostensibly symbolized by the imperial monarchy in Vienna was whittled away – periods of peaceful stability nothwithstanding – by the national and religious differences encompassed within the Habsburgs' polyglot realm. A constant underlying theme of the period is the sequence of elaborate and uneasy political manoeuvres between the Catholic-dominated Habsburg Empire and the German-speaking states to the north and west; the gradual coherence of those states into a confederation among which Prussia, for the most part staunchly Protestant, became the dominant force; and the difficulty that these two neighbouring power-blocs – despite their largely common language – had in coexisting peacefully. At the same time the nineteenth-century Austrian Empire's official spirit of the age was characterized (as in Russia) by an unswerving policy of preserving the imperial status quo, however implacable the long-term force of events to the contrary.

These events embraced the Europe-wide spate of revolutions in 1848, including one in Vienna, whose destabilizing effect continued to reverberate throughout the years after the immediate restoration of the ruling conservative order. An era of deepening social change, too, had been set in motion by the industrial revolution, with its creation of a liberal-minded urban middle class and, no less significantly, of a nationalist-minded urban working class. The ascendancy of Franz Joseph I to the Habsburg throne in 1848, at the age of eighteen, ushered in what was to become the long final act of this drama of the fall of imperial eagles. The new emperor, who was to rule for sixty-eight years until his death in 1916, single-mindedly dedicated his life to the pragmatic maintenance of the dynasty and the state. He was to remain undeflected from this sober vision by such humiliations as the loss of the remaining Italian states (in whose defence he had fought as a young officer); the victory of Prussia over the Empire in the Seven Weeks' War of 1866, and the associated cession of yet further territory; and the establishment in the following year of what was effectively the dual state of Austria–Hungary under the single rule of the Habsburg monarchy. Far from damping internal nationalist fires, this constitutional and administrative contrivance inflamed them yet further. From now on until the outbreak of the First World War in 1914, the clamour of nationalistic Czech, Polish, Balkan, and Hungarian voices was increasingly insistent and uncompromising.

Webern in 1902 therefore found himself in the capital city of a German-speaking community whose situation within the last remaining remnant of Habsburg Empire was at once central and anomalous. The Austrians spoke the major language of the Empire, and they had long been accustomed to being its most prosperous community. Having for centuries been in this position of apparent security, they had felt little need to organize into a nationalist political bloc, as the Czechs and Hungarians increasingly had throughout the nineteenth century. Yet the background of terminal imperial decline was inescapable; and with the edifice of Habsburg rule beginning to crumble, where could the Austrian Germans look for a continuing sense of identity? Their instinctive linguistic bond with the powerful, recently unified Germany to the north was complicated by deep historical and cultural differences. At the same time, the rise of the two main Austrian class-based political parties, the Social Democrats and the Christian Socials (in response to the past century's changing social pressures), had not in itself addressed this uncertain sense of nationhood. Uncertainty breeds irrationality; and irrationality breeds a particular kind of resentment against other communities whose social structures appear both alien and more secure.

Vienna, like every major city in eastern Europe, had a large Jewish community; by 1890 it amounted to eleven per cent of the city's population. On the whole it had integrated closely into the German-speaking society around it, and its members had become strikingly successful within the city's administrative and commercial circles. Meanwhile the extent to which the Jews had already become a near-automatic target for unfocused racial prejudice is evident in one of the first letters that Webern wrote to Ernst Diez after the start of his first university term.

In the course of a detailed description of his impressions of the cosmopolitan city, his university courses, his tutors, and his fellow students at the Musicological Institute where he had recently enrolled, Webern remarked: 'The members of the institute include seven Jews, a Jewess, four Poles and four Germans ... When I went to the institute for the first time I shuddered at the many difficulties. I would have liked best to quit right then, the Jews were all so unfriendly, etc. By now, I have already grown used to it.' The remark surely says more about Vienna than about Webern himself (the earnest new arrival from provincial Klagenfurt, apprehensive at the start of university life in the big city, desperately keen to mix with the other students and say the things that they were saying, and who had probably barely spoken to a Jew in his life before). But the fact that this and other similar references in his letters at the time were almost certainly made unthinkingly shows – perhaps more revealingly than a more conscious display of prejudice would have shown – the ingrained depth of the malaise to which Vienna had already succumbed.

One of the agreeable aspects of life in Vienna, then as now, was its burgeoning musical activity. Webern plunged into this with his usual enthusiasm, and soon found that such a rich diet was at times too much even for him. 'Now the tidal wave of the concert season roars with terrible force,' he wrote in his diary. 'Too much, too much! Every day there are at least three concerts …' His impressions of this exciting new world of music-making are interesting in their wide-ranging response. He remained true to his admiration for Wagner and Strauss; re-confirmed Beethoven's prominent place in his personal musical pantheon; added to it the works of the Austrian symphonist Anton Bruckner and the Hungarian composer–pianist Franz Liszt; and roundly berated the general level of Wagner performances in Vienna for failing, in his view, to approach the celestial standard enshrined in his memories of Bayreuth. But he also became interested in non-German exotica of the kind that, in later years, he was to dismiss with contempt. A performance of *Djamileh*, a one-act opera by the French composer Georges Bizet (of *Carmen* fame), made a strong impression on him. 'Music saturated with oriental ardour,' was Webern's reaction, 'full of ingenious rhythm, enchantingly orchestrated. Gustav Mahler conducted. I saw the man for the first time. An artist! Long black hair, closely shaven face, eye glasses. How he leads the orchestra! He extracts everything from the score.'

Meanwhile, besides his regular studies in musical history and theory at the university, Webern was also busy with work of a kind which, unknown to him at the time, was to be the deepest and most lasting influence on his own music. In charge of the Musicological Institute at the university was Professor Guido Adler, an authority on medieval and Renaissance music. Part of Webern's course consisted of lessons in transcribing this music out of the ancient notation in which it was originally written down (which is difficult for non-specialist performers to read) and into the standard modern equivalent. At first denouncing this task to Diez as 'a horribly dry and troublesome chore', Webern soon found himself enthralled by the music of the Renaissance masters – pre-eminently Josquin des Près, Johannes Ockeghem, Heinrich Isaac, Pierre de la Rue, and Jacob Obrecht – who flourished around the turn of the fifteenth and sixteenth centuries.

Following page, Vienna, where Webern studied from 1902 to 1906; view towards the city centre from the northwest, with the Stephansdom (St Stephen's Cathedral) in the distance.

In the set of lectures on modern musical history that he was to give thirty years later, Webern referred collectively to these composers as 'the Netherlanders'. It is a correctly approximate definition, in that while most of them came from the region stretching across what is

now northern France, from Flanders and the Netherlands to Burgundy, they also travelled and worked widely throughout Europe (especially in Italy). Accordingly there is no such thing as a single predominating style of Renaissance choral music; the individual creative personalities, and the range of cultural influences on each, are as strikingly varied as in later generations. What *is* different about this music compared to that of subsequent centuries is the way in which it works technically. Most of it was written for voices, in most cases almost certainly unaccompanied. The human voice, though a uniquely expressive resource, cannot achieve the range and virtuosity of performance which was to be made possible by technical developments in instrument-building in subsequent centuries – developments whose culminating product was the nineteenth-century symphony orchestra, with whose repertory Webern was now eagerly acquainting himself in Vienna. Relatively restricted resources of performance meant that technical developments in Renaissance choral music proceeded differently: in the direction of an unparalleled sophistication of compositional device.

It is not possible to appreciate the radical fusion of the old and the new that was to occur in Webern's music without some discussion of the way that these devices function. The best place for this, however, is in relation to each work of Webern's where the influence of his beloved 'Netherlanders' is immediately clear. Besides, he himself can at first hardly have comprehended how their way of composing might relate to his own compositional concerns. But it is clear that he already sensed something significant for him in this music, whose distilled style and intricate purity of technique were a world away from the dazzling, feverish musical bazaar that was turn-of-the-century Vienna.

In the preceding few years Webern's composing had proceeded only sporadically, hampered – so he had complained to Diez – by study for his final examinations in Klagenfurt and then, at least to start with, by his exacting workload in Vienna. Composition exercises were a required part of his university course, however, and so with his usual industry he set about fulfilling what his tutors expected of him. The process clearly did him good, as he now began to branch out into other musical genres besides that of voice-and-piano song-settings. During his first two years at Vienna University

Guido Adler, Webern's
professor of musicology at
Vienna University,
photographed in 1927

Webern produced a considerable number of short piano pieces,
movements for string quartet, and orchestral arrangements of other
composers' music: songs by Schubert and Wolf, and some of
Schubert's piano sonatas. Much of this work did not, on Webern's
own admission, inspire him very much, but he undoubtedly
recognized its usefulness in extending his compositional armoury.

He continued to think of his song-settings as his 'real' music, and
found them easier to compose during his holidays at the Preglhof,
well away from the demands of university work. His songs now
began to develop a more consciously exploratory style than before;
several deploy an increasingly intense chromaticism to unleash a
mood of Wagnerian vehemence, expertly extending the late-
Romantic, Wolfian idiom in which Webern was already so
accomplished. He also jumped feet first into rather less refined
territory with an orchestral arrangement of *Siegfrieds Schwert*
('Siegfried's Sword'), a heroic ballad by the German composer and
singer, Martin Plüddemann.

The founder and leading light of his self-styled *Balladenschulen*
(ballad schools) of composition, Plüddemann, who was born in

Kolberg (now Kołobrzeg) in 1854 and died in Berlin in 1897, was a famous figure in his time. From 1889 to 1894 he lived and worked in Graz, and it is therefore very likely that this is where the pre-teenage Webern, then also living there, first came across Plüddemann's sturdily Teutonic ballad settings for voice and piano. *Siegfrieds Schwert*, to a text by the nineteenth-century German poet Ludwig Uhland, was a celebrated example of these; and the nineteen-year-old Webern's enthusiastic response to its folk-like, unsophisticated tone now resulted in a splendidly boisterous arrangement for a full-sized orchestra. Having got the idea out of his system in such rousing style, Webern chose not to repeat what can be perceived, with the advantage of hindsight, as a divertingly un-Webernian experiment.

His main effort for the next summer turned out to be an altogether finer achievement. *Im Sommerwind* ('In the Summer Wind'), which Webern subtitled an 'Idyll for large orchestra', was his first serious attempt at a substantial musical structure of this kind. This does not prevent it from being an unpretentiously remarkable work in its own right. Webern found the idea for this quintessential creation of his early nature-worshipping years in a poem of the same name by the North German writer and philosopher Bruno Wille. Instead of setting it vocally, he took the various sections of Wille's lyrical hymn to nature as the basis of his own symphonic design.

It is easy to point to *Im Sommerwind*'s few signs of immaturity. The most prominent is a melodic style too short-breathed to sustain the work's quite large-scale paragraphs so that, instead of sweeping along in the implied Straussian flood, the music seems rather to chase its own tail. There are also a few passages where the instrumentation is so sparse that the music seems momentarily in danger of falling into a hole. (Given the precisely judged spareness that was to be such a feature of Webern's mature style, much has been made of the extent to which this quality is anticipated in the more thinly scored passages of *Im Sommerwind*. It is more of a moot point than the apparent connection might suggest; the stylistic agenda of the earlier work is, after all, quite different.)

But these limitations are only noticeable in the context of the astonishing assurance and command of the Idyll as a whole. Its finest passages – the quiet glow of the opening and closing sections for divided strings, for instance – haunt the ear with an understated

Opposite, a page from Webern's manuscript of Im Sommerwind, 1904 – a late-Romantic work already revealing a personal voice

strength that is, indeed, a Webernian trademark. The orchestral line-up, too, is interesting. Webern specifies a large woodwind and brass section, with six horns instead of the usual four (to add an extra degree of warmth) but, intriguingly, without the normal three trombones and tuba, whose weight of tone might have seemed appropriate to the music's fervent Wagnerian climaxes. Only a detail, maybe; but it shows that, even at this early stage, something within Webern was instinctively seeking a path beyond the glutted sumptuousness that was the Achilles' heel of the late-Romantic orchestral style. Already, in this work, he had created a musical dream-landscape in which the Carinthian countryside itself seems to sing with a loveliness so complete as to be almost poignant.

Im Sommerwind is dated 'Preglhof, 16 September 1904'. A few weeks later, in Vienna, Webern met Arnold Schoenberg.

2

A self-portrait by Arnold
Schoenberg, Webern's mentor
and composition teacher,
painted in oil in 1910

*I wrote the chorus six years ago under your direct
guidance during the year when I last came for
lessons with you. I would like to tell you again
how beautiful the memory of those times is for
me. I believe that I can still recall every one of
your words. I believe I can remember each single
lesson. All that you told me is of immeasurable
value to me … And whatever happens to me in
life, I will at once orient my conscience towards
you. Thus it shall remain for ever. You are set up
in my heart as my highest ideal whom I love
more and more, to whom I am more and more
devoted.*

Webern to Schoenberg, June 1914

Schoenberg 1904–8

It is interesting, in the light of Webern's later obsessive dedication to the art of composition, that he did not at first see his future unfolding in quite this way. Throughout his upbringing in Klagenfurt he had set his sights on a broadly based musical career of which composing was to be only a part. At the age of sixteen the young musician was already playing the piano for rehearsals of the men's choral society in Klagenfurt, and he was by then also a sufficiently fine pianist and cellist to be working on difficult solo parts from the concerto repertory, evidently playing them well enough for a professional career as a soloist to be at least a possibility. Meanwhile his trigger-happy readiness to denounce what he considered to be poor performances of opera or orchestral works had been matched from the start by a determination to do better himself. He dreamed of becoming a conductor, and believed that his best chance of success was to keep up his cello and piano studies during his university years, then to join one of the great German or Austrian opera houses or symphony orchestras, and graduate from the ranks to the conductor's podium. He therefore continued to take private cello and piano lessons alongside his university studies, and worked away at the development of his multiple musical skills with his habitual thoroughness.

Already, however, his dissatisfaction with the routine tasks set for him by his university tutors, combined with a deepening urge to compose, had led him to start looking for a more inspiring mentor. By the spring of 1904 he had satisfied himself that Mahler, who was pursuing a frenetic double career of composition during the summer holidays and a non-stop conducting schedule for the rest of the year, would hardly have had the time to take on private pupils even if he had wished. Webern consequently decided to seek out another major musical figure of the age: Hans Pfitzner.

Pfitzner's music has made little headway outside the German-speaking world. Its posthumous reputation for oppressive Teutonic conservatism over-simplifies the achievement of an uneven composer whose finest work – such as his opera *Palestrina*, completed in 1917 – reveals a profound and idiosyncratic relationship to the music of the past. Pfitzner, like Webern, was always to believe absolutely in the artistic validity of the German Romantic tradition. Unlike Webern, he was not to feel impelled to develop the style and technique of his own music beyond the existing syntax of that tradition. Pfitzner already regarded Mahler, for instance, as a dangerously modernistic presence. Even so, Webern's choice of potential teacher was not as surprising, at this early stage of his development, as posterity has tended to make out. The twenty-year-old musicology student saw himself as an idealist rather than as an iconoclast, and the Wagnerian provenance of the two operas that Pfitzner had already composed at this time must have indicated a potential kindred spirit. One of Webern's fellow students in Vienna, Heinrich Jalowetz, evidently felt the same way. Having persuaded Guido Adler to secure them an audience with Pfitzner, the two friends set off for Berlin, where the German composer had a teaching position.

A woodcut caricature (by Hans Lindloff, 1908) of the composer Hans Pfitzner, who proved too conservative a figure for the young Webern in search of a teacher

    The encounter seems to have gone well enough to start with. It went less well when Pfitzner made the fatal error of making clear that he did not share young Anton von Webern's opinion of the music of Gustav Mahler. Webern's response was that in that case, he and the distinguished composer fourteen years his senior had nothing further to discuss; he got up from his chair, took Jalowetz by the arm, and marched both his friend and himself out of the room. Musical history is therefore left with one of its more intriguing question-marks. Supposing Webern, instead of reacting in his usual intemperate manner, had for once managed to contain himself, that the interview had gone well, and that he had indeed begun to study with Pfitzner. How would his own work have turned out? It cannot automatically be assumed that it would *not* have developed as it did; Webern's voracious appetite for new experiences would have been bound to lead him to encounter Schoenberg's music sooner or later. On the other hand *Im Sommerwind* was to be completed only a few months after Webern's meeting with Pfitzner, and its gifted young creator would surely have found much to learn from the senior composer's singular brand of masterful traditionalism. Might Webern's beautiful early symphonic poem have turned out to be the first of a number of successors? Any clues as to whether, on a better day, his encounter with Pfitzner might have turned out differently are lost in the unrecorded conversation between two music students – one, we may imagine, still simmering with ungovernable rage, the other genially attempting to calm him down – as their train rattled along the railway line back to Vienna. Webern appears never to have discussed the subject again.

It will by now be clear, from even the most sympathetic assessment, that Webern's was not an easy personality. One of the side-effects of a nature that makes extreme demands on itself is that that same nature tends to make its possessor difficult company for others. Yet Webern had an instinctive capacity for making friends and, with exceptions, keeping them; also his choice of friends, again with exceptions, was usually excellent. Heinrich Jalowetz's constant support for Webern, often during the most difficult periods of the composer's life, is one of the happier stories to punctuate the years to come. The friendship seems to have been an excellent double act, with Webern's compulsive and dedicated idealism interacting happily with Jalowetz's good-humoured companionship. A viola player with, at this time, an interest in composing, Jalowetz was to go on to develop a successful conducting career in opera houses throughout the German-speaking world. Also – as was to be true of several of Webern's close and long-standing friends – he was Jewish.

Along with their colleagues at Vienna University, Webern and Jalowetz assembled for the start of the new academic year in October 1904. Webern, still restlessly casting around for a composition teacher, came across an advertisement in a Viennese newspaper announcing extra-curricular courses in musical instruction, to be given for the second year running at the Schwarzwald School by one Arnold Schoenberg. Possibly Webern was alerted to Schoenberg's activities in the school's self-styled 'free conservatoire' by Guido Adler; contrary to the image implied by his distinguished academic position, Adler was interested in new musical developments and is known to have encouraged some of his other pupils to attend Schoenberg's classes. In any event, the first encounter between the professor's star musicology student and the Schwarzwald School's charismatic composition teacher was to change Webern's life in a single, decisive stroke.

Arnold Schoenberg, a
photographic portrait taken
in his forties

Schoenberg had been born in Vienna in 1874 to Jewish parents.
His mother's family came from Prague, where her ancestors included
a long line of synagogue cantors; his father, who owned and ran a
shoe-shop, was from Pressburg (now Bratislava in Slovakia). At the
age of thirty, despite a poor if not destitute upbringing and a
virtually self-taught musical education, Schoenberg had already
made his mark as the most controversial composer of his time.

Gifted with unquenchable self-belief, phenomenal physical and
mental energy, a riveting personality already remarkable for its
combative forcefulness, and a relentless capacity for hard work,
Schoenberg had been composing fluently, if haphazardly, since the
age of eight. When he was fifteen his father died, and the music-
obsessed youngster had to help support his family by working in a
bank. In 1893 he was one of the two cellists in an amateur Viennese
orchestra whose rehearsals were taken over by a rising young
composer–conductor, Alexander von Zemlinsky. The older man gave
Schoenberg the only instruction in composition he was ever to have,
while also helping to widen his musical horizons, so that the young
cellist–composer added an understanding of Wagner's and Bruckner's

First page of the manuscript
score of Schoenberg's
Verklärte Nacht for string
sextet (1899), a work
exploring dangerously new
harmonic territory

advanced chromaticism to his existing knowledge of Brahms, Beethoven and Mozart. Two years later the bank at which Schoenberg worked went into liquidation, and he exuberantly flung himself into the first of what were to be many temporary musical jobs: in this case, conducting a metal-workers' choir in Stockerau, a village on the northern edge of the Danube valley some twenty kilometres upriver from Vienna, to and from which Schoenberg would regularly walk when he could not afford the fare.

The first of his works that Schoenberg was subsequently to acknowledge were composed at this time: three groups of songs for voice and piano, whose accompaniments explored post-Wagnerian chromatic harmony with sufficient insistence to cause a *frisson* of unease among their first Viennese audiences. Then in September 1899, while on holiday with Zemlinsky, he wrote in just three weeks a major work which combined, with unprecedented originality, the genres of chamber music and symphonic poem. This was the rapturously beautiful *Verklärte Nacht* ('Transfigured Night'), scored for the unusual medium of string sextet – two each of violins, violas, and cellos, a combination twice used before by Brahms – and based on a poem by the well-known late-Romantic German writer, Richard Dehmel. Zemlinsky submitted Schoenberg's early masterpiece for performance in Vienna. It was rejected on the grounds of dangerously extreme chromaticism, and in particular because it contained a chord which could not be found in any existing musical textbook.

That a creation of such loveliness and subsequent popularity should have met with such hostility before a note of it had even been played hints at the less appealing side of the city which can legitimately claim to be the most musical in the world. Decades pass, wars and empires come and go; meanwhile the Viennese continue to flock to opera and concerts as they have for centuries. What strikes the foreign visitor is the extent to which this appetite for music, in its highbrow and lowbrow manifestations alike, cuts across the barriers of class and income that still tend to prevail in other capital cities. Goings-on, real or rumoured, at the Vienna State Opera or the Musikverein (home of the Vienna Philharmonic Orchestra) really do make national newspaper headlines, and are discussed by the middle and working classes alike with the meticulous passion that other

Following page, the newly built theatre of the Vienna Court Opera in the 1880s. The home of the renamed Vienna State Opera after the fall of the Habsburg Empire in 1918, it was destroyed by Allied bombing in 1944 and subsequently rebuilt to the same design.

nations reserve for football, food, fashion or films. In this respect little has changed in the 100-odd years since Schoenberg's early works burst onto the Viennese musical scene and showed that, then as now, its concert-goers' continuing adoration of the central Austro-German repertory – from Mozart to the Strauss family – tended to pull up short when confronted with something that was disconcertingly different (or which sounded as if it might be). The Viennese knew what they liked, and supported it lovingly. With exceptions, they were equally sure about what they did not like.

This at once endearing and exasperating resistance to change needed little encouragement to harden into vicious hostility, as Schoenberg and his circle were to spend the next half-century finding out. Others had already done so. When the theatre of the Vienna Court Opera (now the State Opera) was completed in 1869, criticism of the new building's design was so unremittingly savage that its architect eventually committed suicide. (The Viennese today point out the huge State Opera theatre with its spectacular façade as one of their city's proudest landmarks.) In 1897 a similar *Skandal* was stirred up by the young artists of the 'Vienna Secession' who, with the painter Gustav Klimt as their father-figure, literally seceded from the

Viennese scandals were provoked by, *left*, a building in the Michaelerplatz designed by Adolf Loos, and, *right*, the art of the Secession. The Secession Building, shown here in a poster designed by Josef Maria Olbrich, opened in 1898 and displayed works such as, *far right*, Gustav Klimt's *Watersprites I*, painted in oil c. 1904–7.

Left, Sigmund Freud,
Viennese father of modern
psychology, photographed
in 1909
Opposite, the seamier side
of life was probed in the
dramas of Arthur Schnitzler,
right, and Frank Wedekind
(*far right,* a scene from
Wedekind's *Schloss
Wetterstein,* Berlin, 1925,
with Karl Bildt and Pamela
Wedekind, the playwright's
daughter).

establishment-minded Künstlerhaus – where their work had been systematically rejected – and set up their own alternative exhibition-space, just as the French Impressionist painters had started up their 'Salon des Refusés' in Paris some years earlier. Also at this time the architect Adolf Loos was designing buildings in a clean-lined, modernistic style which at once became a further topic of fierce Viennese debate; the plays of Arthur Schnitzler and Frank Wedekind were exposing the seamy underside of life behind the glittering façade of the imperial city; and in science and the humanities, Sigmund Freud's theory of psychoanalysis was proving as contentious at the time of its inception as it remains today.

The backdrop to this ferment of cultural activity was the glittering architectural splendour of the Habsburgs' capital, which must already

have seemed an impossibly grandiose visual symbol of an empire in the final stages of political decline. Much has been made of the city's *fin-de-siècle* decadence and incipient social decay at this period, perhaps unreasonably; there is no evidence that life behind Viennese closed doors was any more Babylonian than it is in most cities at most times in their history. It was the incongruousness of the contrast between the visible trappings of imperial grandeur, and the under-lying sense of the writing being on the wall, that seemed so extreme to the sharper minds in Viennese artistic circles. But within those circles there was also an equally strong mood of 'new age' optimism and confidence; and meanwhile the bulk of the city's music-loving populace had lost none of its appetite for dancing the night away to the Strauss family's latest batch of waltzes and polkas. This is the music, trapped in its effervescent, turn-of-the-century time-warp, which seems most truly to sum up the phenomenon which was and is Vienna: Vienna with its German love of high culture suffused with an unmistakably Latin flair for enjoying itself, and shot through with an inexhaustible capacity for intrigue, rumour-mongering and character-assassination.

Schoenberg, sure enough, had already been demonized in established musical circles as the man who wrote music containing chords which did not exist, and whose exquisitely expressive *Verklärte Nacht* had been rejected for performance with the comment that 'it sounds as if someone had smeared the score of [Wagner's] *Tristan* while the ink was still wet'. Schoenberg's response was to start work on his gigantic cantata *Gurrelieder* ('Songs of Gurre', eventually to be completed in 1911) while supplementing his meagre living as a choral conductor by orchestrating other composers' operettas. In 1901 he married Zemlinsky's sister, Mathilde, and – exasperated by the lack of recognition accorded him in his native city – took a job at a cabaret theatre in Berlin. While there he made contact with Richard Strauss, who at that time was conductor of the Berlin Court Opera; Strauss, impressed by the draft score of *Gurrelieder*, encouraged Schoenberg to compose an opera based on the play *Pelléas et Mélisande* by the Belgian writer Maurice Maeterlinck, whose symbolist-influenced work was then much in vogue. Although apparently unaware that the French composer Debussy had just completed an opera based on the same play, Schoenberg instead decided to use Maeterlinck's drama as the subject of a symphonic poem for large orchestra. Rather than drawing on the mood of veiled symbolism and understated tension typical of the play, and similarly of Debussy's opera, Schoenberg's *Pelleas und Melisande* raised the Austro-German late-Romantic style to new and formidable heights of fevered orchestral rhetoric and technical complexity.

When Schoenberg returned to Vienna in the summer of 1903, *Verklärte Nacht* had at last been played; its première in March 1902, given by an augmented string quartet led by the violinist Arnold Rosé, had been noted for the undercurrent of hissing that persisted during the performance, thus marking out the occasion as a *Skandal* of the authentic Viennese variety. (It will not, of course, have escaped the attention of sections of the audience that Schoenberg was Jewish, and so was Rosé.) Webern did not hear *Verklärte Nacht* then, but he did attend a repeat performance in the autumn of 1903. In the interim he had also looked through a score of *Pelleas und Melisande* – then still unperformed – which a fellow student had brought along to the university. Though he was intrigued by both works, there is no evidence that Webern was unreservedly bowled over by either of them at this stage. (A few years later he was to write to Schoenberg maintaining that he had indeed been so smitten; but given the by then well-established nature of the Webern–Schoenberg friendship, it can be submitted that Webern either would have felt compelled to say this, or may conveniently have allowed his memory to deceive him.) What was about to change Webern's entire view of his own musical future was not so much Schoenberg's music as Schoenberg's personality.

The power of that personality now proceeded to attract some of Vienna's brightest young musical talent as moths are drawn to a candle-flame. Webern, overwhelmed by his first encounter, immediately asked to be taken on as a private pupil, and was soon joined by Heinrich Jalowetz and other new recruits. A significant event was the arrival at the self-proclaimed 'School of Schoenberg' of a young civil servant by the name of Alban Berg. Having been forced into his uncongenial profession by parents who doubted his musical talent, Berg – the future composer of two masterly operas, *Wozzeck* and *Lulu* – owed this change of fortune to his own elder brother, who had seen Schoenberg's newspaper advertisement and had sent a selection of his

sibling's already copious output of songs to Schoenberg without
Berg's knowledge. Webern and Berg became instant and close friends.
They were to remain so despite their different natures – the tall,
handsome, urbane, charming Berg was in almost every way the
antithesis of the short, bespectacled, impulsively serious Webern –
and their equally dissimilar artistic personalities.

Schoenberg's view of what he expected from his pupils was quite
straightforward: he demanded absolute personal dedication and
loyalty, unstinting support for his own embattled but increasingly
prominent career as a composer, and wholehearted submission to his
methods of instruction. The nature of that instruction was very
different, however, from the dogmatic rigidity of the traditional
conservatoire system, some of whose graduates had already had such
trouble coming to terms with the theoretical basis of Schoenberg's

Detail from a portrait of
Webern's close friend, the
composer Alban Berg,
painted in oil by his teacher
Schoenberg, c. 1910

Webern, photographed in
his late twenties

ARNOLD SCHÖNBERG

MIT BEITRÄGEN VON ALBAN BERG
PARIS VON GÜTERSLOH · K. HORWITZ
HEINRICH JALOWETZ · W. KANDINSKY
PAUL KÖNIGER · KARL LINKE
ROBERT NEUMANN · ERWIN STEIN
ANT. V. WEBERN · EGON WELLESZ

R. PIPER & CO · MÜNCHEN 1912

ARNOLD SCHÖNBERG
Nach einer Amateur-Aufnahme

Frontispiece and title page of the Schoenberg symposium *Der Lehrer,* edited by Webern and Alban Berg

'non-existent' chords. Contributing some years later to a collection of Schoenberg-admiring testimonials entitled *Der Lehrer* ('The Teacher'), Webern wrote:

> *Before all else, Schoenberg demands that the pupil should not write just any notes to comply with a school formula, but that he should perform these exercises out of a necessity for expression. Consequently, he actually has to create, even from the most primitive beginnings of shaping a musical syntax. All of what Schoenberg then explains to the pupil, on the basis of the latter's work, results organically from it;* he brings no doctrine to it from without. *[Author's emphasis] Thus, Schoenberg actually educates through the creative process. With the greatest energy he searches out the pupil's personality, seeking to deepen it, to help it break through – in short, to give to the pupil [in Schoenberg's own words] 'the courage and the strength to confront things in such a way that everything*

he looks at becomes an exceptional case by virtue of the way he looks at it'. This is an education in utter truthfulness with oneself. Besides the purely musical, it embraces also all other spheres of human life. Yes, truly, one learns more than rules of art with Schoenberg.

The last two sentences hint at the change that was now to come over Webern's personality. For all his violent likes and dislikes on matters to do with Art in general and with Wagner and Mahler in particular, his way of responding to the world around him could not reasonably be described as unbalanced, let alone pathological, until Schoenberg came into his life. It can be argued that Webern's personality, genuinely strong in itself, was to be irreparably warped by this prolonged exposure to one yet stronger, and that – however deeply his music was to benefit from Schoenberg's uncompromising artistic idealism and pedagogic brilliance – Webern's attitude to Schoenberg himself was disturbingly redolent of the 'master and slave' syndrome. This does not seem due to the fact that Schoenberg was some years older than Webern; indeed, as time went on, they were increasingly to view each other as colleagues, rather than as teacher and pupil. Nonetheless, the relationship in its early stages did Webern's nature much harm, and beyond doubt affected the younger man's ability to conduct his life with the no-nonsense practicality required to make a success of a career as a working musician, however gifted. It is tempting to wonder whether Webern the man might not have lived less frenetically if he had settled for studying with Pfitzner while the opportunity existed. But then we would probably not today have the music that Webern the artist left us; and one suspects that, given a chance to live his life over again, he would not have considered the psychological traumas that were ceaselessly to punctuate the creation of that music to be a matter of much consequence. After all, one must live only for Art.

Webern now proceeded, with redoubled intensity, to do just that. Working relentlessly hard throughout his four years of tuition under Schoenberg, by 1908 he would already have composed well over 100 pieces of music including unfinished individual movements and technical exercises – a remarkable total, considering that his university studies would have been enough to keep many another conscientious student fully occupied. Early casualties of this punishing schedule

were his formal piano and cello studies; for a performing musician
to keep his or her fingers in trim for a professional career, several
hours of daily practice are normally required, and with both
Schoenberg and Guido Adler now putting the young musicologist–
composer through the mill, this was no longer a realistic option for
Webern. Besides, he was now quite sure of his destiny as a composer.

Schoenberg evidently realized from the start that Webern was an
artist blessed with almost *too* much talent – one of those whose
superabundant compositional skills are liable to get in their own way
unless their possessor learns how to channel them to maximum effect.
With his natural and unteachable gift as a song-composer, Webern
was evidently going to learn little from Schoenberg in this area that
he would not discover on his own. Instead, the master set about
raising the pupil's less developed expertise in instrumental composition to a similar standard. The issue, as Schoenberg saw it, was that
whereas a verbal text suggests possibilities as to the overall shape of its
musical setting, a piece of music without a text does not start off with
this advantage. Its structure has to evolve from scratch.

By the late eighteenth century Western classical music had already
evolved a number of standard forms (forms, that is, in the sense of
flexible principles of musical argument, rather than fixed structural
moulds into which musical ideas could merely be unimaginatively
poured). These included sonata form, where two or more contrasting
ideas or groups of ideas are stated, developmentally sparked together,
and then restated to round out the movement; the verse-and-refrain
design of rondo form, concerned with the play and release of ideas
rather than, as in sonata form, with their drama-generating
engagement; and variation form, where an initial idea is decorated,
extended, and otherwise varied as the movement's central basis.
(There are intriguing parallels here with ethnic musical forms such as
the North Indian raag and the Scottish pibroch.) For all his
radicalism in matters of style, Schoenberg believed that every
composer needed to understand how to handle these traditional
forms; the more exploratory and boundary-stretching musical
language was becoming, he insisted, the more important it was that
the technical and structural articulation of that language must be
securely based. He therefore set Webern to composing one instrumental movement after another, mostly for string quartet or for solo

strings and piano. The results could easily be tried out in performance by Webern and his fellow students; and chamber music, which side-steps much of the complex science of instrumentation involved in composing an orchestral score, is an ideal medium for concentrating on musical essentials.

Some of Webern's more substantial efforts of these years have been published, and they give a vivid idea of the eagerness with which, on Schoenberg's instructions, he kept setting himself new structural and musical problems to solve. A single slow movement, known by its German name of *Langsamer Satz* and completed in Vienna in June 1905, is an exercise in late-Romantic soulfulness; its underlying mood of sweet serenity looks back to the tranced, dream-like mood of *Im Sommerwind* as well as forward to a new, leaner style that Webern was already developing. This sense of Janus-like transition is more pronounced in the String Quartet of 1905, which was written mostly at the Preglhof that summer and finished in September while Webern was staying at the nearby home of Ernst Diez and his family. Laid out in a sizeable single movement, this altogether more ambitious piece contains an unmistakable portent of Webern's later style: its very opening presents a three-note figure – not so much a theme as a self-contained musical cell – which immediately becomes the central developmental source from which the work's entire trajectory springs. The Quartet also adventurously explores the colouristic sonorities obtainable from stringed instruments: the ethereal, glassy sound of high harmonics; the use of mutes to veil the instruments' tone; plucked notes, as distinct from those played with the bow; the nasal effect induced by bowing near the bridge of the instruments; the fluttering sound of tremolo bowing; and various combinations of all these. The result is an intense, twilit sound-world vividly influenced by that of *Verklärte Nacht*. Most of these sonic devices turn up in music of earlier periods (Mozart's deployment of muted string sound, for instance, is wonderfully imaginative). But the frequency and density of their use in *Verklärte Nacht* was a new departure whose possibilities were not lost on Webern.

Significantly, too, both these early string quartet essays have autobiographical connections. Almost every work that Webern was ever to compose related directly to some aspect of his personal experience. The *Langsamer Satz* was his creative response to a holiday he and Wilhelmine Mörtl took together in the spring of 1905 when they visited the Waldwinkel in Lower Austria, a famously pretty stretch of countryside about sixty kilometres west of Vienna, much favoured by nature-loving Viennese snatching a short break from city life.

The young couple spent five idyllic days hiking westwards up the valley of the river Kamp from Rosenburg to Zwettl, and then cutting northeast across the Waldviertel hill country and down to Allentsteig. Webern later wrote of the trip in his diary, impressing himself with the kind of over-the-top literary flourishes to which artistically and romantically smitten 21-year-olds tend to be vulnerable. 'We wandered through forests,' he wrote. 'It was a fairyland! High tree trunks all around us, a green luminescence in between, and here and there floods of gold on the green moss. The forest symphony resounded … A walk in the moonlight on flowery meadows – Then the night – "what the night gave to me, will long make me tremble." – Two souls had wed.' The quotation is from a poem by Detlev von Liliencron which Webern had already set to music in 1903, and it hints at the nature of the deepening love between Webern and his adoring cousin. So does another diary entry written a few months later at the start of the annual family summer holiday at the Preglhof. Much as Webern loved the house and its surrounding countryside, these evidently did not altogether compensate for Wilhelmine's absence. 'Now I am separated from her,' he wrote. 'I am in the solitude of forests and mountains, and my soul longs for her, for her love. O, could the wings of my yearning carry my love to her! How painful parting is!'

His loneliness did not, however, prevent him from getting down to work on his new String Quartet. This was inspired by the *Trittico della natura,* depicting *La vita* ('Life'), *La natura* ('Nature') and *La morte* ('Death') through the seasons of the year, painted by Giovanni Segantini, whose powerful mountain landscapes had much impressed Webern. In November 1904 he had heard a performance of Beethoven's 'Eroica' Symphony in Vienna, and his post-concert impressions had considered the connection he sensed between the composer and the painter who at this time were twin pinnacles of his inspiration.

I long for an artist in music such as Segantini was in painting. His music would have to be a music that a man writes in solitude, far away from all turmoil of the world, in contemplation of the glaciers, of eternal ice and snow, of the sombre mountain giants ... The onslaught of an alpine storm, the mighty force of the mountains, the radiance of the summer sun on flower-covered meadows – all these would have to be in the music, born immediately out of alpine solitude. That man would then be the Beethoven of our day.

Webern had penned these thoughts only a few weeks after his first encounter with Schoenberg, for whom the identification of musical inspiration with nature was at best incidental, and who no doubt had already forcibly said so to his impressionable pupil. But while Schoenberg was to undermine the independence of Webern's personality in other ways, his overbearing nature impinged not at all on the deeper artistic ideas of the younger composer. The diary extract above could have been written at any point in Webern's life. And while it is difficult to detect with certainty any literal cross-references between the String Quartet of 1905 and Segantini's triptych, they will undoubtedly have existed in Webern's own mind.

Before the start of the new university term Webern travelled to Munich in order to put in some extra-mural research for his degree course by visiting some art exhibitions. A notebook dedicated to Wilhelmine recorded his impressions of these and other experiences, among which was a performance of Wagner's *Die Meistersinger von Nürnberg* ('The Mastersingers of Nuremberg') conducted by one of the foremost maestros of the age, Arthur Nikisch (whom Webern nonetheless berated for taking the opera at 'incredibly fast' tempos). He was much more impressed by *Hidalla*, a play by Frank Wedekind, with whose denunciations of bourgeois sexual morality Webern had decided he resoundingly identified. His notebook duly listed 'the greatest barbarisms of our culture: (a) the old spinster (what could be uglier than an old maid, for the sole reason that she is unnatural to the highest degree?) (b) the high esteem accorded to virginity before matrimony (c) the contempt and persecution levied on the whore.' This was followed by a withering diatribe against the bourgeoisie 'whose malice stinks like a cadaver! ... Lazy, immovable, full of dullness, without emotion, without enthusiasm, without courage,

Giovanni Segantini, *La morte* ('Death') from the *Trittico della natura*, 1898-9, which inspired Webern's String Quartet of 1905

they waste away and do not perceive beauty.' (One imagines the tranquil Wilhelmine conscientiously reading through her lover's latest verbal artillery barrage, and perhaps wondering whether he included her own lawyer father as a fully paid-up member of this pestilential tribe of bourgeois 'peasants'.) His indignation expressed to his satisfaction, Webern interrupted his journey back to Vienna by stopping off for a few days' exploration of the Salzkammergut region, staying at the lake of Alt-Aussee, whose enchanting, mountain-encircled setting rapidly restored his good humour.

Returning to Vienna for the start of the new term, he flung himself into his final year's university studies. The major project was his doctoral thesis in musicology, for which he had selected part of the *Choralis Constantinus* of the Flemish-born Renaissance composer Heinrich Isaac as a suitable subject. (In the German-speaking world it was normal, then as now, for university doctorates to be awarded at both graduate and postgraduate level.) Isaac's huge three-part work, composed at around the turn of the fifteenth and sixteenth centuries, consists of unaccompanied choral settings of the individual sections of the Proper of the Roman Catholic Mass – the Proper being a liturgical text (with a related plainchant as its musical basis) specific to a particular feast-day or saint's day, as distinct from the sections of Kyrie, Gloria, Credo, Sanctus, Benedictus, and Agnus Dei which together make up the daily Ordinary of the Mass. Webern opted to study and edit the music of the second part of Isaac's magnum opus, and it is a measure of Guido Adler's respect for his young undergraduate's abilities that he considered Webern to be up to such a task. The fruits of these labours were eventually published in 1909 in Volume 32 of *Denkmäler der Tonkunst in Österreich* ('Memorials of Musical Art in Austria'), the monumental edition of early music

The lake at Alt-Aussee,
visited by Webern in 1905

Title page to the tenor part
for the first of three volumes
in Heinrich Isaac's *Choralis
Constantinus,* posthumously
published in 1550.
The second volume was
the subject of Webern's
doctoral dissertation.

PRIMVS TOMVS

TENOR

CORALIS CONSTANTINI, VT

vulgo vocant, opus infigne & præclarum, vereǫ cœleftis harmoniæ, Authore nunquá fatis lau-
dato Mufico, Henrico Ifaac, Diui quondam Cæfaris Maximiliani Symphonifta Regio, opus
inquam, illuftris Ifaci, officina dignum, & propter compofitionis artifitium, & cygneam
venuftatem, adeo vt ex fæcundifsimo tanti artificis pectore, vere
emanaffe videatur.

Nornbergæ imprimebat Hieronymus Formfchneider
Cum gratia & priuilegio Cæfareæ Maieftatis ad quinquennium.
Anno 1550.

supervised by Adler. Webern's contribution consists of edited transcriptions of Isaac's twenty-five settings of the office of the Mass Proper (amounting to 194 closely packed pages of musical score) along with a meticulously researched introduction examining the work's liturgical sources and assessing its technical and artistic splendours.

With his thesis safely submitted by June 1906, Webern had the more immediate problem of coping with the intimidating workload for his final examinations. Ernst Diez helped him with some unofficial coaching in art history as the examination dates approached. Webern's mood of anxiety was not helped by Wilhelmine's absence in Geneva, where she had recently been sent by her family for three months to brush up her French. He became even more nervous when one of the two professors assigned to assess his thesis, doubtless bewildered by the extent of its expertise and scholarship, declared it incomprehensible and threatened not to approve it. Fortunately the other signatory was Adler himself, who succeeded in bringing round his recalcitrant colleague. The examinations themselves went successfully, and by the end of July the newly graduated Dr Anton von Webern was back at the Preglhof for a well-earned summer holiday.

He had somehow managed to continue his studies under Schoenberg during this final university year, and must now have been looking forward to a few months' untroubled composing at home in the Carinthian countryside. It was not to be. Some years beforehand Webern's mother had developed diabetes, in those days (before the discovery of insulin) still an incurable disease. During the summer months her condition steadily worsened, and she died in September at the age of fifty-three.

While Webern never really got over her loss, his grief was of the kind that retreats inside the heart and stays there, emerging only in the occasional reference in a letter to a friend and in other, deeper ways. Six years and several remarkable compositions later, Webern was to write to Alban Berg that 'except for the violin pieces and a few of my orchestra pieces, all of my works from the Passacaglia on relate to the death of my mother ... the Passacaglia, the String Quartet, most of the songs, the Second Quartet, the first orchestra pieces, and the second set (with a few exceptions)'. He tantalizingly did not

The Webern family grave in the churchyard at Schwabegg as it looks today. The inscription across the two walls reads 'Freiherrn von Webern'. The memorial plaque to Webern's mother is on the far left.

specify whether this was equally true of the music he was to compose before his Passacaglia of 1908, after which he appears to have dismissed virtually all his previous works as unrepresentative fore-runners. (*Im Sommerwind*, for instance, was never performed in Webern's lifetime, entirely by his own choice.) Perhaps this was because, in his own mind, the connections between his pre-Passacaglia works and the memory of his mother were insufficiently close to deserve the wider recognition that performance and publication might bring.

For years his mother's death shrouded Webern's life in an enveloping nightmare which, while it spurred his creativity to develop at an astounding rate, simultaneously damaged his capacity to cope with the world around him, sometimes to a desperate extent. Her grave in Schwabegg's village churchyard was to remain for him a place of constant pilgrimage. Not even Wilhelmine's love could console him, as she herself implicitly acknowledged in a letter written to Webern at Christmas 1906. In it she seems to accept a role which many a lover and wife-to-be, finding herself relegated emotionally to second-best status, would simply have refused to fill. But Wilhelmine was neither as independently minded nor as selfish as that. 'My love cannot replace for you the love of your mother,' she wrote, 'but it will help you to create a beautiful life. And to assist you in reaching the highest goal as man and artist is the most beautiful content of my own life. I want to preserve your mother's memory in you.'

Traumatized as he was, Webern had to confront his postgraduate future. With his musicology doctorate under his belt, he could probably have secured an academic post almost anywhere in the German-speaking world if he had really wanted to. Instead, his determination to pursue a career as a conductor now forced its way again to the surface. He had also convinced himself that his destiny lay not in conducting an orchestra, but in the opera house. His attempts over the next two years to secure a foothold in the Austrian and German opera-house network seem to have been unproductive, although he may have done some coaching work at the Vienna Volksoper (the city's second opera house after the Court Opera) where Zemlinsky – who would already have known Webern through his brother-in-law, Schoenberg – was now principal conductor. Webern's father had meanwhile agreed to make over a regular allowance to his son until he had found a steady conducting post.

Consciously or otherwise, Webern now took advantage of this financial lifeline as an opportunity to immerse himself in his continuing course of study with Schoenberg. The previous year's main achievement had been a Rondo for string quartet, an attractive work with a swinging, waltz-like main theme, whose Viennese tunefulness nonetheless sits uncomfortably alongside the music's abundance of restless chromaticism. This by now familiar problem for Webern – of making musical means and ends coincide – remained unresolved in the single existing 'first movement' of a Piano Quintet (i.e., for solo piano and string quartet) which he completed in the spring of 1907. The weighty, Brahms-derived style of the piano writing seems counter-productive, especially in relation to the music's wilder harmonic excursions. But it may be that the idea was not Webern's alone. ('You haven't tried something in the style of Brahms. Write something in the style of Brahms.' 'Yes, Mr Schoenberg.') Webern always retained a fondness for his Quintet, and in the 1930s even thought about publishing it, a step he apparently did not consider with his other early creations.

In none of these had he come much closer to solving the musical conundrum preoccupying him. How was he to develop the option of building large-scale musical paragraphs through a melodic style which, far from wanting to expand, seemed to insist on pulling inwards? The knack of generating large structures out of a style crystallizing in short phrases is – among the great composers of the German symphonic tradition – unique to Mahler, a creative sleight-of-hand of which Webern must have been frustratedly aware. The problem did not exist for Schoenberg, who composed naturally in long, Brahmsian lines and had already mastered the art of combining this linear fluency with post-Wagnerian, very un-Brahmsian chromatic harmony. It may have begun to dawn on Webern at about this time that if his music was so reluctant to expand outwards, perhaps that was because something within it was gravitating in a quite different direction: inwards, towards greater concentration.

However fitful his progress as an instrumental composer, his song-writing gifts meanwhile flowered wonderfully in the Five Songs after poems by Richard Dehmel. The first of these had been composed early in 1906; two years later Webern completed the cycle which proclaims him as the finest Lieder composer to have emerged since Hugo Wolf. Dehmel, the author of the poem that had inspired Schoenberg's *Verklärte Nacht*, was a leading standard-bearer in the crusade being mounted by many of the leading German and Austrian artists of the day against the stifling bourgeois values they perceived to be festering around them. His work had therefore earned Webern's firm approval, and it now brought out the very best in the young song-composer. The five texts deploy Webern's preferred genre of nature-imagery to enhance the poet's exploration of a world of Romantic emotionalism at once passionate and rarefied. Webern's music perfectly captures this mood of suspended emotional animation; the lean, chiselled, beautifully worked piano writing and restrained vocal line together operate within a harmonic sound-world which, while pushing at the limits of conventional tonality, does so with a subtle poise reminiscent of Gabriel Fauré, the contemporary French master of the *mélodie* (the French counterpart of the voice-and-piano German Lied). Indeed the affinity is so striking that one wonders whether Webern had in fact heard and liked any of Fauré's songs. What is beyond doubt is that the new tone of asceticism in the Dehmel Songs points clearly to the pared-down directness of utterance that was to dominate Webern's mature style.

Meanwhile the main product of the year 1908 was an orchestral Passacaglia which Webern proudly designated 'opus 1'. It can legitimately claim to be the most masterly opus 1 ever composed. In a musical world nowadays obsessed with all things Mahlerian, neo-Mahlerian or post-Mahlerian, the Passacaglia would surely have become more popular than it has if Webern had given it a more colourful title (rather than the dryly descriptive kind he was always to prefer).

The passacaglia form, as Webern deploys it, is essentially a variation form, based on the short theme announced with maximum simplicity at the work's opening. There follow twenty-three intricately worked variations and a developmental coda (or tailpiece), assembled into a near-seamless musical flow whose cumulative power shows how impressively Webern had learned to build a genuinely large-scale musical structure. The music's turbulent emotionalism and its undertone of tragedy are each unmistakably Mahlerian. Schoenberg's influence is evident both in the 24-year-old Webern's superlative technical command of his material, and in the concept of a single one-movement form, rather than the traditional multi-movement symphony, as a vehicle for a major instrumental statement of this (abstract) kind. Webern may have derived the idea from Schoenberg's one-movement First Chamber Symphony of 1906 – a formidable, hyperactively inventive creation whose first performances had outraged Viennese audiences two years previously. (In the winter of 1922–3 Webern was to make an expert arrangement of Schoenberg's chamber-orchestra original for an ensemble of five soloists.)

With the Passacaglia down on paper, Webern now convinced himself – or had been convinced by his ever-patient father – that it was high time he found a 'proper job' as an opera conductor. So began a long litany of disastrous attempts to establish himself in a profession for which, given his anti-pragmatic idealism in everything to do with Art, he could hardly have been temperamentally less suited. At this time he started to compose an opera – *Alladine und*

Following page, Bad Ischl as it looked in 1908, when Webern worked there during the summer at the theatre

Palomides, based on a play by Maeterlinck – but completed only a fragment of its prelude before abandoning the idea. Then, in July 1908, he was offered the post of coach, chorus master, and assistant conductor at the theatre in Bad Ischl, a spa town in the Salzkammergut.

Webern had no sooner arrived than he was writing to Ernst Diez that a visit from his cousin 'would lighten my stay in this hell. My activities are horrible. I find no words to describe such a theatre … What benefit would be done to mankind if all operettas, farces, and folk-plays were destroyed … But through hell into purgatory and finally into heaven – such is the path I must travel.' Since he did not specify the reasons for his disgust, it is entirely possible that someone working in the theatre had merely said something rude about Mahler (or Schoenberg). At all events, by November he was back in Vienna for the première of his Passacaglia, which he conducted himself in a concert of works by the 'School of Schoenberg' in the Musikverein. The press reviews were mostly hostile, the consensus being that the pernicious influence of Schoenberg on his fellow members of the 'High School of Dissonance' was ruining the undoubted talents of Webern and his colleagues. That Webern's conducting was not, however, adversely commented on by the ultra-critical Viennese press attests at least to its competence.

Viennese hostility towards the Schoenberg circle was even more pronounced a few weeks later, when Schoenberg's Second String Quartet was premièred by the Rosé Quartet. 'Scandal in the

Mahler, a loyal supporter of the Schoenberg school, photographed, *right,* in Vienna, 1904; his conducting – represented, *below,* in silhouettes by Otto Böhler – was an inspiration to the young Webern, 'How he leads the orchestra! He extracts everything from the score.'

Bösendorfer Hall!' proclaimed the headline in one newspaper, reporting on the medley of hissing, laughter, strategically timed sneezing, and cries of 'Stop! Enough!' that had emanated from the auditorium throughout the performance, to be countered just as fiercely by the shouts of Schoenberg's supporters (naturally between movements rather than during them). It had been much the same story at every recent Schoenberg première. That of *Pelleas und Melisande* in 1905 had precipitated a mass audience walkout (with one member earning applause for his conspicuous departure by the emergency exit). Mahler, ever a loyal supporter of the Schoenberg school despite his confessed bewilderment at the complexity of their music, had been in the audience at the première of Schoenberg's First String Quartet in 1907, where he furiously informed the nearest contributor to the storm of post-performance abuse, 'You have no right to hiss!' (To which his opponent replied, 'I hiss at your symphonies too.')

Mahler's ten years at the helm of the Vienna Court Opera had recently been brought to an end by a long series of administrative intrigues; he was conducting in America at the time of the Second String Quartet's première, at which his presence might possibly have prevented some of the audience's more unsavoury excesses. 'They are going to play Beethoven now – you had better have the hall aired,' shouted someone to Ludwig Bösendorfer, the distinguished head of the famous piano-manufacturing firm that ran the hall. The press reviews that appeared over the next few days were, with few excep-tions, vitriolic. 'The composition is not an aesthetic but a patholo-gical case,' read one. 'Out of respect for the composer we will assume that he is tone-deaf and thus musically *non compos* ... Otherwise the Quartet would have to be declared a musical public nuisance, with its author brought to trial by the Department of Health.'

It is not surprising that attacks of this kind had the effect of making the members of the Schoenberg circle close ranks even more determinedly than they would have anyway. Neither Schoenberg nor Webern were ever to express any doubt as to the validity of the direction in which their music was heading, and their unwished-for sense of creative isolation served only to deepen this unassailable belief in the rightness of their cause. Before departing for Christmas at the Preglhof after this latest débâcle, Webern wrote to Schoenberg:

'I am still totally upset and now am trying to remove from my thoughts this unspeakable, horrible experience, so that I can think again quite clearly about your exceedingly beautiful work. To me it is a marvel.' Writing again a few days later he added: 'Nothing is now more important than showing those pigs that we do not allow ourselves to be intimidated.'

Everyone in Vienna knew, of course, that a string quartet is a string quartet, so the introduction of a solo soprano voice in Schoenberg's Second Quartet must have seemed deliberately provocative. The work's last two movements are settings of texts by Stefan George, the German poet whose mystically speculative beliefs and writings, much influenced by the French symbolist poets such as Mallarmé and Baudelaire, were at this time a major topic of interest among progressive cultural circles in Vienna. 'I feel the air of another planet,' began the poem that Schoenberg set in the finale of his Second Quartet. The words exactly symbolize the point to which his music, like Webern's, had now developed, where the harmonic language was so advanced that it seemed on the verge of breaking away from conventional tonality altogether.

Webern, too, had just made a setting of another George poem celebrating this sense of musical and spiritual release from the bonds of artistic and material convention. His *Entflieht auf leichten Kähnen* ('Take flight in light barques') for unaccompanied chorus – the last

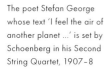

The poet Stefan George whose text 'I feel the air of another planet ...' is set by Schoenberg in his Second String Quartet, 1907–8

work he wrote under Schoenberg's tutelage – remarkably combines an idiom of supple, lilting, disembodied melodic and harmonic expressiveness with a method of construction taken from Renaissance choral music: it is written entirely in strict counterpoint, using the techniques of canon and double canon. (Counterpoint – or polyphony, i.e., 'many voices' – is the art of simultaneously combining two or more independent melodic lines so that their interaction generates the music's sense of onward motion. Canon consists of taking a single melody and singing or playing it several times at once while phasing in each successive repetition, so that the tune literally combines with itself to generate a multi-layered, self-sufficient musical structure. Children's songs sung by two or more different groups starting their melodies at different times operate on exactly the same principle. For Webern, like the Netherlanders before him, complex results could be generated by combining melodic lines running at different speeds, by beginning each of these at a higher or lower pitch, or by using inverted or reversed variants of the same material. The technique is as much rhythmic – concerned with the precise interlocking of the musical cogwheels of each phrase – as melodic.)

Like Schoenberg's Second Quartet, *Entflieht auf leichten Kähnen* is an exceptionally beautiful creation. It also shows how, quite independently of Schoenberg, Webern was already drawing on his own technical and artistic resources to find a way of navigating musically in this new and bewildering harmonic world – a world towards which, without realizing it, the two composers had for years been travelling. The quiet chord on which *Entflieht auf leichten Kähnen* alights at its close is the final outpost of traditional tonality in Webern's work – the last visible promontory of a familiar land, slipping now behind the horizon as a serious, bespectacled, disconcertingly intense musicology graduate set his course unflinchingly towards the uncharted musical seas ahead.

3

An ink drawing of Webern, made
by Oskar Kokoschka in 1912

*Your quartet touched my father deeply. He also
liked Berg's sonata. My pieces are too 'nervous'
for him. 'It is always all over before it starts,'
he says.*

Webern to Schoenberg, July 1912

Into the Unknown 1908-14

Webern's need to find and maintain a conducting post was now made more urgent by his father's decision, prompted by failing health, to resign his post at the Ministry of Agriculture, give up the family flat in Vienna, and retire to the Preglhof. Webern accordingly went job-hunting in Berlin – unsuccessfully, though he made the most of his visit by twice going to hear Debussy's opera *Pelléas et Mélisande*, by whose understated, anti-rhetorical idiom he was greatly impressed. Debussy's music, he wrote to Schoenberg, was 'very fine, often very strange, in places wonderfully beautiful … such atmosphere, such tenderness, then again so much passion … The new stage art is something quite glorious, and therefore I must stay with the theatre.'

Claude Debussy, the composer of *Pelléas et Mélisande*, an opera which Webern heard twice in Berlin, 1908, and much admired

Five months previously Webern had written to Ernst Diez from
Bad Ischl about his planned opera *Alladine und Palomides* – to be
based, like Debussy's masterwork, on a Maeterlinck play. Responding
to Diez's evident readiness to write the libretto, Webern had informed
his cousin that 'I need nothing but a few characters. By no means a
theatrical piece. To a certain extent Maeterlinck writes in this vein.
But I want it even more so. Just to get away from everything that is
now called theatre. The opposite … If your libretto turns out that
way, then it will be all right with me. Everything else repulses me to
the highest degree.' On one level these remarks may have been
influenced by the immediate circumstances of Webern's detested
summer job at the theatre in Bad Ischl. But they are also strikingly
reminiscent of Debussy's radical approach to opera in *Pelléas et
Mélisande*, an approach summed up in the French composer's
pronouncement that 'in the opera house, they sing too much'. In
the light of the late-Romantic rhetoric which still dominated
Schoenberg's music at this time, and considering Schoenberg's
strident resistance (with rare exceptions) to the products of any
musical tradition outside the German one, it is intriguing that
Webern appears to have been developing his own version of the
Debussyan concept of anti-opera well before he had heard a note of
Pelléas et Mélisande, and quite regardless of his teacher's predilections.

That Debussy's influence on Webern was not, in the event, to
result in the creation of an opera does not make that influence any
less profound; on the contrary, the Debussyan example of the power
of musical understatement was a revelation that informed everything
he was to compose from that time on. (Nor did his preoccupation
with the theatre ever quite leave him. Years later, when a pupil asked
him if he would ever contemplate composing an opera, he is said to
have replied 'If I live long enough and find a good text.') Back in
Vienna after his trip to Berlin, Webern set to work on a number of
further settings of poems by Stefan George – this time for voice and
piano – on which the influence of Debussy's *Pelléas* is unmistakable.
In the two sets of five songs each that Webern later decided to
publish, the music operates at an almost constant hushed *pianissimo*,
as if striving to capture the clenched, subdued emotionalism of
Debussy's opera (and of George's poems) in his own now fully
chromatic style. The manner of the remaining four settings, which

were published only posthumously, is more vehement, which perhaps explains why Webern decided to hold them back.

His life was now to be dominated by two themes which combined in far from harmonious counterpoint: attempt after disastrous attempt to establish himself as an opera conductor in one theatre after another, and creative developments in his and Schoenberg's music which accelerated at bewildering speed. During a spring holiday at the Preglhof in 1909 Webern turned again to the string-quartet medium. By mid-June he had completed his Five Movements for String Quartet, a work whose deadpan title belies the eruptive forces which now exploded to the surface in his music.

The frosted-glass hypersensitivity of the George songs is transformed in the Five Movements into a new and alarming world of convulsed Expressionism, articulated in contrasts of pace, volume, and tone-colour so violent that they threaten to split the music apart. The musical phrases themselves are unprecedentedly concentrated and terse; the colouristic devices familiar from Webern's earlier string-writing are developed to new extremes; and the five disconnected movements – respectively manic, depressive, manic, depressive, and depressive, all of them either very fast or very slow – make no attempt at the kind of integrated musical statement traditionally implied by the term 'string quartet' (which is why Webern did not formally call it that).

Since this is the point in history where, for many listeners, classical music started sounding like modern music – i.e., dissonant, 'atonal', or just plain mad – it is worth emphasizing that these developments did not take place in a vacuum. 'Atonal' is a word which literally means 'not in any (traditional) tonality'. It has stuck to the music of the Schoenberg circle like a burr; but it is nonetheless a meaningless way of describing the idiom of, say, Webern's Five Movements, since it does not describe what this music *is* 'in' instead. Schoenberg was subsequently to propose 'pantonal' – i.e., music in every tonality at once – which is hardly more illuminating. A more accurate definition might be 'extended tonality', or 'suspended tonality' (suspended in both senses of the word), or 'total chromaticism'; but adjectives such as 'extendedly-tonal' are too unwieldy to be practicable.

Whatever the appropriate semantics, it takes only the first few seconds of listening to Webern's Five Movements – or to Schoenberg's Three Piano Pieces Op. 11, composed at around the same time – to sense at once that something unsettling did happen to music early in 1909. It was as if Schoenberg and Webern had for years been paying out a tonal sheet-anchor so that their music could roam freely, yet also still quite securely, on an increasingly turbulent harmonic sea, only to find one day that the sheet-anchor had been paid out to such a distance that it had suddenly ceased functioning as such, and that their music was now swirling about as if this stabilizing device were no longer there. No wonder they felt bewildered, and that most listeners still do, when encountering the results of the two composers' first ventures into these uncharted waters. Familiarity helps; so does a willingness to hear the music as sounding entirely like itself, as distinct from not sounding entirely like Mozart.

On one level the Five Movements were composed as an elegy for Webern's mother: a study in choked, drowsy, almost narcotically numbed grief, flaring into desiccated shrieks of horror and despair, or reverting equally unpredictably to a mood of wistful valediction. Heard from a different angle (for instance in a different performance) the work comes across in another way, as an all-too-vivid evocation of the dispiriting side of life in turn-of-the-century Vienna. This is the music of bare, fusty, unheated rooms; of pale street-lamps in cold, bitterly windswept streets; of the hideously bleak sense of inner emptiness and isolation that the artist, like anyone else, periodically has to confront and endure.

Unexpectedly, a few weeks after Webern had completed the Five Movements, a conducting opportunity materialized for him in Innsbruck in North Tyrol, where the local theatre needed an assistant conductor. Webern had been there only a few days when, exactly as in Bad Ischl the previous summer, something happened to make him explode in a mood of idealistic outrage only thinly disguising a catastrophic loss of nerve. 'By God, dear Mr Schoenberg, it is impossible for me to remain here,' he wrote in a near-hysterical missive to his ex-teacher. 'It would be a sin against the Holy Ghost … And anyway, what do I have to do with such a theatre? O my God, do I have to perform all this filth? … The change was too sudden – I cannot endure this. Please, Mr Schoenberg, send me a few lines –

Innsbruck, in the early
1900s, where Webern
worked, briefly, in 1909

Hotel Grauer Bär, Innsbruck. I am sure to die here. I am being murdered here. Your Webern.' To judge from a version of events that Webern described to a pupil many years later, Schoenberg replied by quoting the Swedish author Strindberg at him: 'Cancel out and keep going!' If this was Schoenberg's way of telling Webern to pull himself together and get on with his life, it did not work. Three days later Webern was back at the Preglhof, still in a bad state, but not bad enough to have prevented him from stopping off on the journey home to climb a magnificent mountain in East Tyrol. 'Today I came down from the Hochschober,' he wrote to Schoenberg. 'Up there, in the heights, there one should stay.'

Burying himself in his composing once again, within a few weeks he had composed his Six Pieces for Orchestra, music which extends the idiom of the Five Movements for String Quartet into a virtuoso exercise in post-Mahlerian orchestral psychodrama. Again, Webern conceived the work as a memorial to his mother; again, the music's contrasts between frozen despair, wistful evanescence and shrill horror are frighteningly extreme. What is new is Webern's daring handling of a massive orchestral apparatus. This is seldom unleashed at full volume; instead, Webern pursues the widest possible range of tone-colours, parcelling these out from instrument to instrument, a few notes at a time, through and across the music's individual melodic lines so that the effect is of a variegated orchestral mosaic. The procedure is embryonically discernible in Mahler's music, but Webern here developed it with unprecedented radicalism. (Schoenberg was to coin the word *Klangfarbenmelodie* – 'sound-colour melody' – to describe this technique.) All six pieces are strikingly brief except for the longer fourth: a spectral, slow-motion funeral march, proceeding in an ominous hush until suddenly rearing up in a fearsome concluding roar of massed percussion sound. The work as a whole is as deeply remarkable as its mood is deeply depressing. Within less than five years, its creator had journeyed from the sunlit idyll of *Im Sommerwind* to the darkest music he was ever to compose.

The evidence might seem to indicate that artistically, Webern was still hanging onto his ex-teacher's coat-tails. During the winter of 1908–9 Schoenberg composed a voice-and-piano song-cycle, *Das Buch der hängenden Gärten* ('The Book of the Hanging Gardens'), to poems by Stefan George; Webern responded with his own George

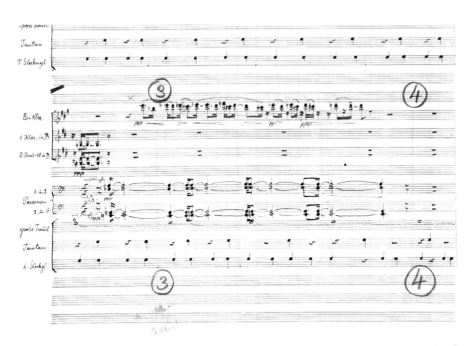

Part of Webern's manuscript of the fourth of his Six Pieces for Orchestra, headed *marcia funebre* ('funeral march') in this original version of 1909

settings. Next, Schoenberg produced his Three Piano Pieces, his first work in which an Expressionist manner pushes violently to the surface; Webern came up with his similarly ground-breaking Five Movements for String Quartet. Schoenberg then composed his Five Orchestral Pieces; as if on cue, Webern produced his Six Pieces for Orchestra. But Webern's part in this creative double act was not as derivative as the chronology indicates. There is no true equivalent in Schoenberg's Five Pieces, for instance, of the Mahler-saturated mood of self-dissolution that dominates Webern's work. What does link the two composers, no longer as master and ex-pupil but now as equal colleagues, is a temporary convergence of stylistic and technical agenda. An intriguing counterpart to their situation had developed in Paris at almost exactly the same time in the work of the artists Pablo Picasso and Georges Braque, who – despite their quite different creative personalities – were now painting Cubist canvases so similar that even experts sometimes struggle to tell them apart. The two artists' styles were shortly to diverge again as widely as they had before; meanwhile, as Braque was later to put it, he and Picasso felt themselves to be like two mountaineers climbing the same rock-face,

roped together on an adventure into unknown territory. Webern and
Schoenberg would have known what he meant.

The extra-musical forces at work in the two composers' lives were
meanwhile very different. Webern's emotional landscape continued to
be haunted by the death of his mother. In 1908 Mathilde Schoenberg
had left her husband and gone to live with Richard Gerstl, a painter
who had a flat in the same block as the Schoenberg household.
Webern was instrumental in arranging a reconciliation between
Mathilde and the upset and outraged Schoenberg, to whom she duly
returned. Gerstl then committed suicide. Art and life do not always
intersect, however, as precisely as is often believed. While it is
possible that Schoenberg's personal trauma in some way triggered the
Expressionist explosion that detonated in his music from 1909
onwards, it is just as likely that this was something waiting to happen
for purely musical reasons alone.

Similarly, anyone encountering Webern's Six Pieces for Orchestra
might reasonably deduce that their creator must have been in a near-
suicidal frame of mind at the time. In fact Webern was in manically
optimistic form: excited at his strengthening creativity, while
irresponsibly ignoring offers of conducting work which various
contacts tried to arrange for him. When he failed even to apply for a
post in Koblenz – an opening engineered for him by Heinrich
Jalowetz – Schoenberg took his ex-pupil to task, eliciting a grovelling
reply which did not, however, change the immediate picture. This
dominating trait of the younger Webern's character – a bizarre blend
of uncompromising idealism and quasi-adolescent naivety – is
amusingly clear from an incident that took place at about this time,
during one of the summer visits with which Gustav Mahler liked to
punctuate his long stretches of conducting in America.

Emerging from the exquisite rural surroundings of Toblach in
South Tyrol (now Dobbiáco in Italy) where he would immerse
himself in composing for a few precious months each year, Mahler
had let it be known that he wished to hold court at an inn in the
Viennese suburb of Grinzing. Webern, who had met the great
composer–conductor through Schoenberg for the first time early in
1905, had at once identified with Mahler's wildly exalted approach to
Life and Art. (It had been the young Mahler who, after the
triumphant public première of Bruckner's Te Deum in Vienna in

1886, scratched out the words 'for chorus, solo voices, orchestra and organ ad libitum' on the title page of his own copy of the score and replaced them with 'for angelic tongues, for God-seekers, tormented spirits and souls purified in flames'.) Webern was present at the little gathering along with Schoenberg, Zemlinsky and younger members of the Schoenberg circle. Mahler, who was doing most of the talking, expounded at length on the subject of Dostoevsky, and expressed his concern at the company's apparent unfamiliarity with the works of the great Russian writer. 'You must change this, Schoenberg!' he proclaimed. 'Let your pupils read Dostoevsky, this is more important even than counterpoint.' Webern timidly raised his hand like a schoolboy and said, 'Please, we have got Strindberg.'

They had indeed; at this time Schoenberg owned forty-four volumes of the visionary, occult-suffused works of the Swedish writer, every one of which he had annotated with his own underlinings and marginal notes. Even Webern, who had (of course) decided that he too admired Strindberg as much as Schoenberg did, could not match this phenomenal appetite for extra-musical cultural research, especially since his own fitful career as an opera conductor now began to take up more of his time. During the following winter season he again worked at the Vienna Volksoper, as before probably at Zemlinsky's instigation. Professional life in an opera house, then as now, involves punishingly long hours; a capacity to cope with semi-permanent logistical and administrative chaos (institutionalized or otherwise); constant clashes with the egos, neuroses and power-plays of conductors, singers, orchestra members and administrators; and, at least in the humble early stages of a career, precious little money to be earned in return for the occasional satisfaction of having had a hand in a performance whose quality makes the long slog of preparation worthwhile. So it is no wonder that Webern composed virtually nothing at this time. When his professional duties prevented him from spending Christmas at the Preglhof, his practically minded father wrote to offer his son some seasoned advice along the lines of not letting his employers at the Volksoper depress his spirits.

Webern's mood became more buoyant when, in May 1910, he secured a more promising job as second conductor at the civic theatre in Bad Teplitz, a prettily located spa town in northern Bohemia. A letter sent to Schoenberg soon after his arrival ominously mentioned

An ink drawing of the Swedish writer August Strindberg by Carl Larsson. Strindberg's work was a major inspiration to Webern and Schoenberg.

how he always hated being away from home, but he does seem to have been genuinely determined to try to make the most of this new opportunity. He got off to a good start with his first conducting assignment, earning a favourable review in the local newspaper, and was looking forward to taking the helm in further performances of the kind of lightweight operetta material which he did not like, but was prepared in the circumstances to take seriously. 'The responsibility heightens the pleasure,' he wrote to Schoenberg. 'The personnel is very nice and does everything I want. I learned much during the winter. I am definitely already on top of things.'

A long and elaborate letter written to Schoenberg three weeks later from Klagenfurt tells, in painstakingly self-justifying detail, the story of the ensuing débâcle. A professional dispute between Webern and one of the singers concerning the previous evening's performance had been referred to the theatre director; the director had taken the singer's side and, when Webern objected, had relieved him from conducting the next performance. Every opera house is an emotional pressure-cooker in which incidents of this kind happen all the time and often blow over quite quickly, as Webern knew perfectly well. Unfortunately he was not one who could bring himself to grin and bear it. Instead, he there and then stormed out of the theatre and, once again, retired hurt to the Preglhof.

A coherent picture emerges quite unmistakably from this sequence of opera-house disasters. What Webern wanted was to compose; he understandably found this impossible when tied down by the exhausting and time-consuming routine of the theatre; and at the back of his mind he knew that as long as his father continued to send him his monthly allowance, he would be able to survive financially without the absolute need to maintain a job. So when the urgency to compose after months of creative silence became extreme, and his separation from his beloved *Heimat* seemed no longer endurable, he knew that unlike others less fortunately provided for, he could always run away from the situation and go home. It is a pity, from a biographer's point of view, that no record exists of the conversation one can imagine taking place between father and son when Webern arrived, somewhat earlier than expected, for his summer stay at the Preglhof.

Ultimately it is not certain whether his behaviour in these
situations should be attributed to a hopelessly misplaced artistic
idealism, or whether it was simply due to a streak of pusillanimous
feeble-mindedness. The relentless demands that Webern made on his
own capacity as a musician, whether as composer, performer or
scholar, indicate that Carl and Amalie von Webern had not been in
the habit of bringing up their children to be spoiled and weak-willed
brats. Nevertheless it is impossible not to sympathize with Webern's
father, who had always taken his son's gifts seriously, and who now
must have begun to doubt whether Webern was capable of rewarding
the faith that had been shown in him.

On his unscheduled arrival at the Preglhof Webern at once settled
down to composing, and within a week had completed a set of Four
Pieces for Violin and Piano. These fearlessly venture deeper into the
territory opened up in the previous year by the Five Movements and
the Six Pieces, with the piano's repertory of subtle resonance-effects
further offsetting the work's angular sound-world of wide leaps and
explosive contrasts. More strikingly still, the music's brevity of form
here becomes a phenomenon in its own right; a performance of the
Four Pieces takes less than five minutes. And Webern's ability
to extract maximum mileage out of his material is now pushed to
the point where a single note can successfully do duty for an
entire phrase.

Having allowed himself, we may imagine, a few idyllic walks in
the Schwabegg countryside to celebrate the speedily achieved creation
of the Four Pieces, Webern was able to write to Berg in mid-July that
he was at work again, this time on 'a big project'. This was *Die sieben
Prinzessinnen* ('The Seven Princesses'), an opera based on a play by
Maurice Maeterlinck, like the abortive *Alladine und Palomides* two
years previously. The manuscript of *Die sieben Prinzessinnen* has
disappeared – exasperatingly, since work on it proceeded much more
fluently than was the case with its predecessor, and it would be
fascinating to know what kind of operatic idiom Webern was now
attempting to evolve. How could the ultra-compressed syntax of his
music at this time possibly have accommodated the necessarily more
spacious dimensions of opera? To judge from the large number of
surviving fragments of earlier compositions, it was not Webern's habit
to destroy unfinished works, so perhaps the torso of *Die sieben*

Prinzessinnen will one day turn up to solve the riddle. In any event
Webern suddenly put it aside for a new and, once again, entirely
different idea. By the end of August he had completed one of the
most astonishing works that even he was ever to compose: the Two
Songs on poems of Rainer Maria Rilke, written for soprano voice and
a chamber group of eight instruments.

The songs are unprecedented in their almost surreal brevity (the
two together last just over two minutes), in their daring re-thinking
of the traditional relationship between the voice and its instrumental
accompaniment, and in the sparseness of their musical idiom. Each
text is set by Webern in a firmly sculpted, yet beautifully supple vocal
line which functions as the connecting thread of the musical fabric,
around which tiny accompanying fragments are woven by the
instrumental group. The total effect is poised, rarefied, wonderfully
expressive, technically as strong as steel, and shows no trace of
speculative experimentalism. Such sure-footed control of an entirely
new style of composing does not come about by chance, and possibly
stems from a musical source which, while light-years distant in one
respect, is closer in others. In his Rilke songs Webern pared down
his spare, Expressionist style to a point where the decorative element
which had been standard in Western musical composition for
centuries was stripped away. Everything is substance. And this is
exactly how the Netherlands choral masters had composed their

The poet and novelist Rainer
Maria Rilke, photographed
in 1903. Webern set two
of Rilke's poems to music
in 1910.

music some 400 years previously. No two styles could actually sound less alike. Yet it is not impossible that – in a deeper sense than anything to do with style – the Netherlanders' music here reached down the centuries to spark across to Webern's.

These wonderful songs also had a more urgent source of inspiration. Both the poems are taken from Rainer Maria Rilke's *Die Aufzeichnungen des Malte Laurids Brigge* ('The Notebook of Malte Laurids Brigge'), a then newly published novel by the German poet. Interpolated as love-songs in the main text, they express in Rilke's lyrical, elliptical imagery the singer's feelings for the object of a love forbidden to be declared to the world. The text details the style of delivery imagined by the poet, who describes the girl's voice as 'strong, full, and yet not heavy; of one piece, without a rent, without a seam', which is exactly how Webern set the two poems. He wrote to Schoenberg that the first one 'compelled me, for it corresponded so completely to my thoughts'. It had reason to. At the moment that he was composing the music, his cousin Wilhelmine was about six weeks pregnant.

It is not clear whether Wilhelmine herself knew this yet; nor is it clear whether, if she did know, she had told Webern. What is entirely clear is that Webern's identification with the subject-matter of the two poems related to the possibility that his and Wilhelmine's relation-ship might at any moment take such a turn. Both their families were staunchly Roman Catholic, and the Catholic Church at that time forbade marriage between first cousins. For that reason alone, it seems surprising that the two sets of parents had allowed the romance to continue for so long. Perhaps they had felt that the best policy was to wait and hope that it would blow over, which made sense when the two lovers were living with their respective families, but rather less sense once Webern had his own apartment in Vienna.

Returning to the city for the start of the new season with, as usual, no regular job in prospect, Webern learned that his friend Heinrich Jalowetz, who was now conducting at the civic theatre in the Baltic port of Danzig (today Gdansk in Poland), had arranged for him to be employed there as an assistant conductor. Webern arrived and launched himself into his work. 'The director is wholly delighted with Jalowetz and me,' he wrote to Schoenberg. 'I conduct several times each week. Thank God that I am at last on the right track.' Sure

Following page, the waterfront at Danzig, the city in which Webern married Wilhelmine Mörtl while employed there at the theatre in the winter of 1910–11

enough, there then followed a replay of the previous summer's happenings at Bad Teplitz, this time complicated by Wilhelmine's desperate situation.

She had gone to Paris to study French, with a view eventually to becoming a teacher. Webern meanwhile wrote a long sequence of despairing letters to Schoenberg, lamenting his thwarted desire to compose, denouncing Danzig ('this strange city that I hate so much'), its theatre and its audience, and apparently shutting from his mind the matter of Wilhelmine's pregnancy for as long as he possibly could. Eventually the lovers had to face reality and inform their disapproving families, both of whom insisted on a church marriage. This turned out to be impossible for first cousins without special papal dispensation, so Webern and Wilhelmine were married in February in a civil ceremony in Danzig, with Jalowetz and his wife Johanna as witnesses. In April Wilhelmine gave birth to a daughter, whom the couple named Amalie after Webern's mother. The arrival of the baby reconciled the older and younger generations in a glow of domestic solicitude, as such happy events are wont to do. (According to Webern's sister Rosa, Carl and Amalie von Webern's first child – a daughter who died in infancy – was born before they themselves were married. If this is true, then Webern's father must have come to realize that he was in no position to point an accusing moral finger at his errant son.) The young family had now set themselves up temporarily in Berlin where Webern, having resigned his Danzig post, set in motion another elaborate quest for a conducting position.

He took his wife and baby daughter with him to the Preglhof for his annual summer stay, and there began to compose a sequence of extraordinarily short and compressed instrumental pieces, some of them literally no more than a few seconds long. Out of this complex genesis was to assemble, over the next two years, a group of works whose hyper-expressive manner is distilled to a point from where, in one sense, Webern could have progressed no further; the next step would have to have been to boil away the last remaining notes and leave only silence. One of many spurious notions with which Webern's posthumous reputation has been saddled is that he cultivated a *fin-de-siècle* aesthetic of silence as 'a living element' in his technique of musical construction. This is nonsense. Composers compose music, not silence, which in Webern's music does what it

does in that of any other composer: it punctuates. But it is true that
the extreme spareness and precision with which the few notes in these
works are deployed does make the ear's awareness of the silence
around them almost supernaturally acute.

Possibly Mahler's death in Vienna in May 1911 accounts for the
poignant tone of some of these marvellously vivid little musical
soundscapes, the early outliers of what were to become the Six
Bagatelles for String Quartet, the Five Pieces for Orchestra Op. 10,
and the Eight Instrumental Fragments. The passing of Mahler, who
in his double career of composer and conductor had literally worked
himself to death by the age of fifty, marked the end of an era, as a
deeply saddened Webern instinctively sensed. But even now, with a
family of his own, his mother's death remained for him the primary
creative impulse. Schoenberg, meanwhile, was also experimenting
with very short and compressed musical forms. In this instance
it was possibly he who was influenced by Webern, rather than the
other way round.

When Schoenberg moved from Vienna to Berlin in September to
give a series of extra-mural lectures at one of the city's conservatoires,
Webern followed. His idea seems to have been to divide the next few
months between teaching private pupils and composing. In fact
his entire winter was taken up in working on behalf of Schoenberg,
whose lecture courses had attracted dwindling audiences after a
promising start, and who was soon in financial trouble. Webern
organized a private fund-raising campaign among the master's
friends and admirers, while also co-ordinating contributions to the
symposium *Der Lehrer* ('The Teacher'). The dowry from
Wilhelmine's parents helped to underwrite this period of unpaid
devotion. Then, in the spring of 1912, Webern received another
financial windfall. His father, who had long since abandoned any
hope of Webern one day being capable of running the Preglhof, sold
the estate and moved to a rented villa in Klagenfurt which he shared
with his two daughters, the older of whom had married and had a
family of her own. The result was that Carl von Webern was able to
make over a considerable sum of money to each of his three children,
so that his son now found himself unexpectedly well off.

Understandably, this did not alleviate Webern's enduring sadness
at losing the house and estate that he loved so much. 'In my memory

it appears to me like a lost paradise,' he was to write to Schoenberg a year later. 'I am overwhelmed with emotion when I imagine everything there as it is now during summer. My daily way to the grave of my mother. The infinite mildness of the entire countryside … If only you could once have seen all this. The seclusion, the quiet, the house, the forests, the garden, and the cemetery.'

As Schoenberg's fortunes in Berlin began to improve, the pendulum of Webern's career began once again to swing back in a familiar direction. 'It is no use,' he wrote to a friend: 'I must conduct … I cannot renounce it. I must perform Schoenberg and Mahler and everything that is sacred.' Once again Heinrich Jalowetz's support enabled him to secure a new job, this time at the theatre in Stettin (today Szczecin in Poland). Events there followed their by now entirely predictable course, with Webern soon describing the theatre (to Berg) as 'this hell-hole of mankind' and its director (to Schoenberg) as 'a cretin beyond compare'. His loathing reached a point where he became psychosomatically ill. His father and his sister Rosa arrived for Christmas to offer some moral support to him and the seven-months-pregnant Wilhelmine, who also had a baby daughter to look after. Mathilde Schoenberg, who also came to visit Webern at this time, found him a physical and nervous wreck who had to hold onto the railing with both hands when climbing the stairs.

Granted some sick leave, Webern took himself off to a sanatorium in Semmering, a beautifully situated resort in the hills to the south-west of Vienna. Told to rest completely, he nonetheless convinced his doctors to let him visit the city at the end of February 1913 for what turned out to be the thunderously successful première of Schoenberg's late-Romantic cantata *Gurrelieder*, in the Great Hall of the Musikverein. Five weeks later, now discharged from the sanatorium, Webern was again present in the same hall for a concert given under the auspices of the Academic Association for Literature and Music. This was to feature the first performances of new works by the Schoenberg circle, including his own Six Pieces for Orchestra. Schoenberg himself was to conduct.

The evening was subsequently reported in a Viennese newspaper by a journalist whose inspired sense of humour ensured that he enjoyed the occasion rather more than did Webern and his colleagues.

The Six Pieces, which began the concert, were greeted by the assembled audience with a heady brew of laughter, applause and
hissing. Zemlinsky's Four Songs on poems by Maeterlinck fared
better; Schoenberg's First Chamber Symphony then provoked 'furious
hissing and clapping ... intermingled, regrettably, with the shrill
tones from house keys and whistles, and in the second balcony it
came to the first fisticuffs of the evening'. (This in the hallowed
Musikvereinsaal, lined with its elegant golden caryatids – the setting
for past premières of Brahms's and Bruckner's symphonies, and of
course of Schoenberg's own *Gurrelieder* just a few weeks beforehand,
at the end of which the composer had been presented with a laurel
wreath.) But the items that turned the concert into a de luxe *Skandal*
even by Viennese standards were two songs from Alban Berg's cycle
setting poems by his friend Peter Altenberg, a sombrely decadent
creation containing some of the most powerful and virtuosic music
that Berg was to compose before his opera *Wozzeck*. Only the first of
the songs had been played, however, when gales of laughter swept
the auditorium.

*However, since Schoenberg stopped in the middle of the piece and
shouted to the audience words to the effect that he would have everyone
disturbing the quiet evicted by means of official force, there erupted anew
agitating and wild invectives, face slappings, and challenges to duels.
Herr von Webern also shouted from his loge that the entire 'baggage' ['das
ganze Gepäck'] was to be thrown out, and from the audience there came
the prompt response that the followers of the disliked musical idiom
should be committed to the Steinhof insane asylum. The raging and
screaming in the hall could now no longer be stopped. It was not at all
unusual to see some gentleman in the audience climb, in breathless haste
and with ape-like agility, over several parquet rows in order to box the
ears of the object of his fury. The intervening police officer could achieve
nothing in this chaos of wildly incensed passions ... Finally, the president
of the Academic Association stepped up onto the conductor's podium
and begged the audience to honour Mahler's memory and listen to his*
Kindertotenlieder *['Songs on the Death of Children']. This ... provoked
somebody to shout a vicious insult, for which the Herr President again
reciprocated with face-slaps. All kinds of people now stormed the*

*Following page, the
Musikverein, home of the
Vienna Philharmonic
Orchestra since 1870, and
the scene of the premières
of Schoenberg's Gurrelieder
and Webern's Six Pieces
for Orchestra*

musicians, who were deathly pale and trembling from excitement. They
exhorted them to vacate the stage and terminate the concert. Nevertheless,
it still took perhaps half an hour before the last rioters noisily left the hall.

Entertainingly as all this reads in retrospect, it was less amusing for
those on the receiving end at the time. Schoenberg's courage in
persisting with the concert for as long as he could displayed his often
misdirected pugnacity at its best; after all, it is one thing to confront
a public riot face to face, and quite another to stand your ground
when your back has to be turned while you try to conduct an
orchestra. Besides, the mood of the Viennese audience was different
from that of the Parisian one which, two months later, was to create
such a commotion at the première of Stravinsky's ballet *The Rite of*
Spring that for most of the time the music apparently could not be
heard at all. The primitivist violence of the Russian composer's score
seems genuinely to have shocked its first listeners. In Vienna, on
the contrary, disrupting the latest concert of the Schoenberg school,
preferably in the most facetious way possible, had by that time
become the thing to do.

Webern's sense of humour, never his strong point, was not
improved by the evening's events. Having already decided not to
return to Stettin, he went with his family (which now included his
six-week-old second daughter, Maria) to Portorose, a spa town near
Trieste on the Adriatic coast, where he had been advised to take
a health cure. From here he wrote to Berg dismissing this latest exhibition by the Viennese public as 'filth', and insisting that he and
Berg must concentrate on writing 'still better compositions' without
worrying any more about such specimens of humanity.

Finding his father's family-filled house in Klagenfurt too noisy
for work, Webern headed for the town of Mürzzuschlag some fifty
kilometres to the southwest of Vienna, where an aunt of Wilhelmine's
ran a butcher's shop. Renting a room high up a nearby mountainside,
he worked on his Three Pieces for String Quartet, climbed the local
Raxalpe, and tried not to think of his forthcoming appointment at
the Deutsches Landestheater (German Theatre) in Prague, where
Zemlinsky had held open a position for him as his musical assistant.
(Not wanting to live in a different town from Schoenberg, Webern
had turned it down the previous year.)

Caricature of *Das nächste Wiener Schönberg-Konzert* ('The next Schoenberg concert in Vienna') in *Die Sonntags Zeit*, 7 April 1913. Schoenberg is conducting; the kneeling figure unceremoniously pushed to the floor in the foreground is Franz Schubert.

In August Wilhelmine took the children to stay with her parents in Vienna while Webern went on reconnaissance to Prague. He managed to rent an apartment before making himself so ill with worry that on his return to Vienna Wilhelmine sent a telegram to Schoenberg, pleading for help. Schoenberg, who was becoming heartily tired of this on-going saga of Webern's opera-house crises, advised him to seek specialist medical treatment. Webern duly submitted to a course of psychotherapy devised by Dr Alfred Adler (no relation of Guido Adler, his erstwhile musicology professor) and gradually began to recover his mental balance, coming to understand, at least momentarily, that his extreme inner demands on himself as an artist had much to do with his inability to face the difficulties and setbacks of a professional career. Adler also seems to have succeeded in temporarily weaning his patient both from the Strindbergian notion that his physical and mental sufferings were predestined, rather than self-induced, and also from his psychological dependence on his ex-teacher; for instead of heading for Berlin and Schoenberg as soon as he could, Webern now stayed on in Vienna. He found a two-room apartment, installed himself, his piano, and the family in it, and despite the cramped conditions settled down to write a Strindberg-influenced play, *Tot* ('Dead'), and also some very fine music.

The impulse behind the writing of *Tot* was the sudden death due to appendicitis, three months previously, of Webern's nephew Theo, the twelve-year-old son of his older sister Maria and her husband Paul Clementschitsch. The drama has four characters: a husband, his wife, a boy representing their dead child, and an angel who brings them celestial consolation. The scenario and its setting fuse, in an exalted visionary conception, Webern's affection for Theo with the two themes that permanently haunted his mind and his music: his memories of his own mother, and his love of the mountains, whose flowers and plants he had already come to identify as symbols of creative beauty and perfection. (The play duly includes a paean to the metaphysical properties of the Edelweiss.) The music he also wrote at this time includes a complete set of Five Pieces for large orchestra; another three pieces scored for a much smaller instrumental line-up, and which he added to two others composed during his last summer at the Preglhof to make up the set which was later published as the Five Pieces for Orchestra Op. 10; and the Three Orchestral Songs of

Opposite, the Raxalpe, which Webern climbed in the summer of 1913, seen from the south

Left, Webern's manuscript
of the first of his Three Pieces
for Cello and Piano, 1914

1913–14, in which a central Stefan George setting is flanked by two songs to poems by Webern himself.

The quality of the Three Orchestral Songs, especially, is so high that the reason behind Webern's refusal to include them among his 'official' works with opus numbers – with a view to publication – can hardly be to do with the music. Evidently he was reluctant to release anything involving his own writings, preferring to keep these away from the public gaze. The second of the Three Pieces for String Quartet written during the preceding summer in Mürzzuschlag consists of another of Webern's poems – a tiny nugget of mother-fixated imagery, just five lines long – set for soprano and string quartet to music of fugitive, spellbinding vividness. Nonetheless he chose to suppress this too. The two outer pieces now became the first and last of the Six Bagatelles for String Quartet, the central four of which Webern had conceived and written down at the Preglhof in 1911 as a self-contained miniature string quartet in four movements. Also dating from this productive period are a number of unfinished attempts at more songs – one of them setting part of Canto XXXI of the *Divine Comedy* by the medieval Italian poet Dante Alighieri. A startlingly terse set of Three Pieces for Cello and Piano was completed in the spring of 1914, as was a more expansive Cello Sonata – expansive by Webernian standards, in that the sonata's single existing movement takes just a few seconds longer to play than the two and a half minutes required by the Three Pieces.

In an introduction that appeared in the published score of the Six Bagatelles in 1924, Schoenberg wrote: 'To express a novel in a single gesture, a joy in a breath – such concentration can only be present in proportion to the absence of self-pity.' The remark pinpoints the quality that raises the music of Webern's so-called 'aphoristic' period far above the decaying stylistic affectation of which it has short-sightedly been accused. Webern could most certainly be self-pitying in his life: yet the ascetic mastery and technical strength of his work tell a very different story. Most of this music was to remain unperformed for several years as its creator forged ahead on his solitary voyage of exploration, his path from now on diverging ever more widely from that of his revered teacher.

In the summer of 1914, life was looking up for Webern. The Viennese publishing house of Universal Edition was showing an

Following page, the arrest
of Gavrilo Princip moments
after the assassination of
Archduke Franz Ferdinand
in Sarajevo, 28 June 1914,
the event that triggered the
First World War

interest in publishing his music; his health had recovered; his composing had been proceeding fluently and well; and he had even made plans to start conducting again at the theatre in Stettin in late August. While on a visit to Klagenfurt in July to see his father, Webern climbed the Hochstuhl, one of the peaks in the mountain range to the south of the city, and sent a rapturous postcard to Schoenberg: 'One of my most ardent wishes is to see something like this with you some day.' His plan to forge up a mountain with Schoenberg in his wake was going to have to wait, however. In June the Archduke Franz Ferdinand, heir to the Habsburg throne, had been assassinated in Sarajevo by a member of a Bosnian group armed by Serbian nationalists (the latest in a series of incidents on the Balkan fringes of the Habsburg Empire which had convinced the imperial government that Serbia represented a major threat to its security). An inexorable sequence of events now unfolded, triggered by the network of alliances in place between the major European power-blocs as a result of decades of complex political manoeuvring since the mid-nineteenth century. On 28 July Austria–Hungary, without having earlier made her intentions fully clear to her ally Germany, declared war on Serbia. Russia mobilized in support of Serbia; Germany declared war on Russia and on her ally, France; and on 4 August Germany invaded neutral Belgium, drawing Britain into the conflict. Europe was at war.

4

*I am striving for the keenest, most exact
understanding of the obligations that have now
become necessary, to relate everything to them, to
live in the most pious submission only to this: to
the rescue and the victory of our fatherland.*

Webern to Schoenberg, June 1916

Anton and Wilhelmine
von Webern photographed in
Mödling, c. 1923

The Singing Heart 1914-26

Historians continue to debate the extent to which the First World War was a cataclysmic accident that could, with a measure of intelligent behind-the-scenes diplomacy, have been avoided. It is probable that the imbalance of power between the great European states – brought about primarily by the massive growth in German military and economic strength following the country's unification in the nineteenth century – would sooner or later have made the conflagration inevitable. In any event, the continent's sudden slide from apparently cloudless peace and prosperity (apart from a few perennial Balkan squabbles) into full-scale mechanized war within less than six weeks caught most of its inhabitants off guard.

Webern, like most of his compatriots, had not realized just how serious the international situation had become. Having given up his apartment in Vienna and paid a sizeable amount of rent in advance to secure one in Stettin, his plans were now turned on their head as the theatre there closed down. Marooned in Klagenfurt with no job and no home of his own to go to, he contacted Zemlinsky at the Deutsches Landestheater in Prague, only to discover that Zemlinsky had of course long since filled the post that he had patiently kept open for Webern the previous year. So the family returned to Vienna, staying once again with Wilhelmine's parents while Webern tried to decide what to do. For once his overriding preoccupation was not with music.

There is nothing like the early part of a war – before rationing begins to bite, conscription throws its net ever wider, and the casualties start to come home – for inducing a nation to surrender itself to a mood of mass patriotic psychosis. Within one week of Germany's invasion of Belgium, Webern was writing to Schoenberg: 'I do not know at all any more how peacetime really was ... I implore Heaven for victory for our army and that of the Germans. It is really inconceivable that the German Reich, and we along with it, should perish. An unshakeable faith in the German spirit, which indeed has created, almost exclusively, the culture of mankind, is awakened in me.'

To point an accusing finger with the advantage of moralizing hindsight is an easy exercise for a later generation, and in many ways a purposeless one. No one who was not actually present in Klagenfurt at this moment in history can be positive that, as a citizen of Austria–Hungary, he or she would not have reacted in much the same way. And no one will normally wish for his or her own country actually to *lose* a war in which it finds itself involved. So a hypothetical friend of Webern's would doubtless have got nowhere by pointing out to him that until mid-1914 he himself had retained, as had most of his compatriots, a measure of suspicion towards Protestant, Prussia-dominated Germany and its motives regarding an Austria–Hungary whose imperial fortunes were on the wane. Nor would it have been much use mentioning also that Webern was someone who lived, by his own proud conviction, only for Art; who had peaceably and assiduously practised what he had preached; and whose awareness of the splendours of his own musical heritage had coexisted with an open-minded response to the equally rich cultural traditions of France and Italy. It is on record that the composer now proclaiming the German spirit's 'almost exclusive' creation of 'the culture of mankind' had heard and liked the Italian composer Gioachino Rossini's effervescent opera *The Barber of Seville* (in Danzig, conducted by Jalowetz), and had also expressed enthusiasm for the music of Rossini's great successor in Italian opera, Giuseppe Verdi. And Webern's interest in French music – Debussy's in particular – had been a major influence on his own work.

None of this made any difference to the cast of mind to which Webern now abandoned himself. The contents of a letter written to Schoenberg in early September show the appalling speed with which an individual of Webern's intelligence can be caught up in the rampant chauvinism of a country embarking on a war. It is as if his articulate, exacting mind – at least as far as artistic matters were concerned – had, like the minds of millions of his compatriots, suddenly become a blank page on which others were free to write. The official propagandists of the already censored Austro-Hungarian press had lost no time in doing so.

Two composers revered by
Webern, their countries and
cultures now divided by the
First World War: *above*,
France's Claude Debussy
and, *right*, Austria's Arnold
Schoenberg, drawn by
Hans Lindloff in 1913

*Do you not agree that this war really has no political motivations? It is
the struggle of the angels with the devils. For everything that has revealed
itself about the enemy nations during the course of these weeks really
demonstrates only one thing: that they are liars and swindlers. Nothing
but infractions of international laws: the apparently long, long
accomplished mobilization of the Russians, the deceitful negotiations, the
bribes among each other, the dum-dum bullets, etc. – what nauseating
filth! By contrast, the open, honourable position of our nations. Lord,
grant that these devils will perish. God indeed ordains it already. This
victory march of the Germans towards Paris. Hail, hail to this people!
A thousand times already I have apologized in thought for having
sometimes been a little suspicious, especially of Protestantism. But I must*

say that I have come closer to it during these times. Catholic France! They have raged against Germans and Austrians like cannibals … And the most ridiculous of all – these Englishmen! They who up to now have only intrigued and who, once they were in battle, ran away so fast that the cavalry could not keep up. Perhaps, as I am writing to you, the Germans are already in Paris. And the Russians, too, will soon be chased away … Oh, everything will end well … The courage of our soldiers in the face of death and their daredevil fighting spirit are said to be without example. If only I could soon take part.

A letter of this kind is not a tablet in stone. In those days it was normal to write letters as fluently as today we speak over the telephone, and all of us say things during long telephone conversations to our friends in intense times that we reasonably might not wish to have quoted back at us later. Schoenberg's attitude to the war in its early stages, too, was broadly patriotic, and Webern had for years been in the dubious habit of writing and saying to his ex-teacher very much what he felt Schoenberg would have wanted him to write and say. Even so, the utter irrationality of the frame of mind revealed in this letter sounds an ominous note of warning regarding the nightmare that was to begin to descend on Webern's country in about twenty years' time. Such things cannot happen except at the behest of a populace of whom large numbers show an aptitude for dedicated and wilful self-delusion. Webern evidently had this quality with capacity to spare.

As the female contingent of the Mörtl household busily knitted woollen socks and mittens for the Habsburg soldiers, Webern considered trying to enlist, but yielded to his family's insistence that this would not be a good idea considering his poor eyesight and, on known form, his far from obvious aptitude for life at the front. So he trained as a male nurse and then, in February 1915, successfully volunteered for non-combatant infantry service, joining a Carinthian regiment based in Klagenfurt which almost at once was posted to Görz (now Gorizia), a town in the Istrian peninsula about forty kilometres north of Trieste. Webern had an austere side to his nature; there was a part of him that thought nothing of spending the night in a mountain hut under the sparsest of conditions before setting out for an assault on a nearby peak before first light, and this taste for spare living now seems to have helped him to adapt to army life with remarkable speed. (The fastidious Berg had also joined up, and – to judge from one of the letters he regularly wrote home to his wife – seems never quite to have recovered from his first encounter with army latrines.)

In May Webern was promoted to corporal and was transferred first to Windisch Feistritz near Marburg (now Maribor in Slovenia), then to Frohnleiten, south of the town of Bruck in northern Styria, where the mountains rising on either side of the Mur valley to the north made him feel at home despite the wartime conditions. In June he was again promoted, this time to the rank of cadet aspirant (equivalent to sergeant), and was put in charge of training some of the older recruits – a task he found he enjoyed, commenting genially to Schoenberg that the process was not so very different from conducting choral rehearsals. ('I try to make everybody take things

Above, Webern (second from right) as cellist of his battalion's 'soldiers' string quartet' in Leoben, autumn 1916

Right, Webern in uniform, photographed during the First World War with Wilhelmine and their daughters Amalie (standing) and Maria

Left, Alban Berg in army
uniform, during the First
World War
Below, Schoenberg in his
army regiment, early 1916;
the composer is seated in
the front row of the company,
second from the right, with
his cap in his hand.

as seriously as possible.') Wilhelmine and the family came out to join him and moved with him when he was yet again transferred, to nearby Niklasdorf – where he played the cello in a string quartet with some uniformed colleagues – and then to Leoben a few miles further up the Mur valley.

Almost everyone in Austria–Hungary at this time had one over-riding priority: that the central powers should win the war. Webern had two overriding priorities: that the central powers should win the war, and that Schoenberg, who had not yet been called up, should be excused military service on the grounds that his capacity for creative work should be protected as a national asset. Schoenberg, whose patriotism made him far from hostile to the idea of enlistment, nonetheless permitted Webern to pursue an assiduous campaign on his behalf. It was unsuccessful, and Schoenberg was called up in December. By then, however, Webern himself was out of uniform.

His sudden disenchantment with the army related in part to his appetite for music once again being whetted by playing in his 'soldiers' string quartet', but the motivation behind his decision once again to approach Zemlinsky in Prague was not only musical. As the prospect of a quick victory over the Allied powers had waned, so the euphoria of the war's early days had waned too. After all (went the general view), Austria–Hungary had only declared war on Serbia; having defeated that country in 1915 and so achieved the required objective, would it not now be possible for the empire conveniently to withdraw from the wider conflict? The answer, as was of course becoming clear to an increasingly hard-pressed populace, was no. On the contrary, Austria–Hungary's embroilment became yet deeper when Italy entered the war on the Allied side in 1915, having secretly been promised substantial territorial gains at the expense of her erstwhile imperial master in the event of an Allied victory. Worse, the empire had been unprepared militarily for modern mechanized warfare on such a scale. While not reduced to the state of tsarist Russia – some of whose 'infantry' were sent to the front armed literally with nothing but the hoes and rakes they used in their fields at home – the Habsburg armies were nonetheless seriously short of weaponry of all kinds, especially artillery. The possibility of the conflict becoming entrenched in an endless stalemate of mutual attrition and slaughter began to dawn on the people of

Alexander von Zemlinsky photographed with his brother-in-law, Schoenberg, in Prague, 1917

Austria–Hungary, just as the same prospect was occurring to the French and British on the western front. Germany, fighting on both fronts, was in no position to help out her weaker ally sufficiently to make a decisive difference to the empire's fortunes.

Webern, as fickle as ever regarding his responses to the world around him, was therefore delighted when Zemlinsky's influence secured his discharge from the army. He went with his family – now augmented by a son, Peter, born in October – to Prague, and assisted eagerly with the musical preparation of forthcoming stagings at the Deutsches Landestheater of Mozart's opera *Così fan tutte* and Schumann's *Scenes from Goethe's Faust*. (Artistic life had been kept going throughout the empire as an officially sanctioned means of shoring up public morale.) Then, in a near-incredible volte-face even by his own standards, Webern decided that he had no right to be enjoying himself in civilian life while Schoenberg was having to endure service in the army, and that therefore he himself must re-enlist. In January he applied to do so without even informing the loyal Zemlinsky, who was naturally furious when he found out. One would like to think that at this point, Wilhelmine too would similarly have informed her adored Toni that enough was enough, and that he and she and the family were staying put in Prague. But even if she did, it made no difference. In early February Webern rejoined the battalion in Leoben and once again embarked on his dual mission of serving the empire and working tirelessly to secure Schoenberg's discharge.

Most of 1916 was taken up with this combination of private and public war efforts. At first Webern was assigned to train younger recruits for the battlefield – a much tougher routine than before, involving strenuous expeditions in the surrounding mountains. Webern's physical fitness proved more than adequate to the task. As the casualties at the front mounted and manpower became in ever shorter supply, it seemed likely that he too might be sent to fight, but an eyesight examination ruled this out. Assigned once again to reserve duties, he played the cello in a chamber group organized by the Leoben battalion's adjutant, whose prominent status in civilian life (at the Ministry of Finance) was promptly deployed, at Webern's insistence, on Schoenberg's behalf.

Following page, Prague, where Webern lived and worked in the winters of 1915–16 and 1917–18

Schoenberg's eventual discharge in October plunged Webern into another phase of disillusionment with the army. Even the prospect of further promotion to the rank of commissioned officer did not raise his spirits. Then, in December, he was declared unfit for further service because of his eyesight, and returned to Vienna where he rented an apartment, settled down to some sustained composing for the first time in nearly three years, and visited Prague with Schoenberg, whose mediating influence may well have played a part in Zemlinsky's offering Webern a post once again at the Deutsches Landestheater, to begin in August. Webern filled in the interim period by staying in his father's house in Klagenfurt, where his creativity continued to flow to his satisfaction.

The family moved once again to Prague, where the winter became very difficult. Food and fuel supplies were desperately short; Webern found himself rehearsing the soloists and chorus for performances of Wagner's *Lohengrin* and *Parsifal* and Mozart's *Don Giovanni* in a theatre which could only be heated in the evenings, so that the hungry musicians worked while wrapped up in their overcoats. Hundreds of thousands of Austrian workers came out on strike to protest against the shortages and demonstrate for peace; the Habsburg fleet mutinied; and while these protests were soon suppressed, the Bolshevik revolution in Russia added a new dimension of instability to the empire's war-exhausted mood. At this time Webern decided that a solution to his and Schoenberg's problems would be to buy a farm with the remains of his Preglhof inheritance; he and the master could then compose there while Webern would also look after the food production on which the two families would live. He told Schoenberg that he had written to ask his father's advice on this. Unfortunately, given Carl von Webern's view of his son's agricultural abilities, the reply is not extant.

In September Schoenberg had once more been called up, only to be discharged again after two months, whereupon he moved to the Viennese suburb of Mödling. Webern's next resolution comes as no surprise: having convinced himself that he was being 'exploited' in Prague, he decided that he too must move to Mödling to be near the master. His father did his best to dissuade him, and even Schoenberg himself, much as he thrived on Webern's hero-worship, insisted that his ex-pupil should stay on in Prague for the time being, if only to support his family. As usual, none of these entreaties made any difference. In April Webern rented an apartment consisting of the entire first floor of a large house in Mödling, to which the family moved three months later. Wilhelmine could have been forgiven for not realizing that this was to be their home for the next thirteen years.

A neutral observer might well have asked how long Webern's bizarre psychological dependence on Schoenberg could continue in this way. Surely something would have to give? Over the next few months it came remarkably close to doing so. Schoenberg, while nonetheless pleased that his acolyte was so willing to be by his side, informed him reasonably enough that he could only offer him a share of his own work at the Schwarzwald School – where his teaching classes were about to resume – and a small remuneration in connection with a new plan: the forthcoming inaugural season of the Verein für musikalische Privataufführungen (Society for Private Musical Performances).

The society's objectives reflected the experience of the Schoenberg circle's pre-war encounters with the Viennese public. Programmes were to be drawn from all schools of composition at home and abroad, and were each to be preceded by an introductory talk; admission was to be by membership obtainable only on annual subscription; the performances were to be exhaustively rehearsed; new works would regularly be played a second time within the same concert; applause afterwards was not to be permitted; critics, recognized or otherwise, were to be allowed to attend only on the strict understanding that press reviews would not subsequently appear; and programmes were not to be announced in advance, so that any existing prejudices would not prevent members from coming. Such a project would depend disproportionately on the dedicated support that Schoenberg expected from his colleagues, and from the start he relied heavily on the expertise of Webern's all-round musicianship, particularly in the art of arranging orchestral scores for the reduced chamber forces to which the society would at first have to restrict itself.

Webern was torn between excitement at this project and the realization that it would amount to prodigious quantities of virtually unpaid work on his part. Predictably, he began to wonder whether he should have left his post in Prague after all. He asked Heinrich

Jalowetz to approach Zemlinsky yet again on his behalf, and in September told Schoenberg how he was thinking. Schoenberg's patience at last snapped. He informed Webern that considering the extensive plans they had been making together for the society's activities, he was fed up with having to discuss the vagaries of Webern's erratic career as an opera conductor. Berg, who had long mastered the art of observing the weathervane-like swings of the Schoenberg–Webern friendship at an amused half-distance, commented in a letter to his wife, Helene: 'Now the most incredible thing has happened. Something that I would not have believed possible any more than, say, that Lloyd George had travelled to Berlin

Above, oil painting by Schoenberg of a *Garden in Mödling,* the Viennese suburb where Webern and Schoenberg both lived in the early 1920s
Left, Ink drawing of Schoenberg by Egon Schiele, 1914

in order to smother Kaiser Wilhelm with kisses: Webern has served notice on Schoenberg – quite simply, with a few words – of the termination of their friendship.'

Webern promptly took his family to stay with his parents-in-law in Vienna while he looked for somewhere else to live. The seriousness of the rift was clear to Berg, who at this time had resumed his civil service career and was working at the Ministry of War in the city. Finding himself effectively in the position of go-between, he wrote to his wife: 'The comical aspect of the matter is that Webern naturally cannot find an apartment in Vienna and is moving back to Mödling again today, and that he does not know how he can avoid meeting any of the Schoenbergs, who, as you know, live in the closest vicinity … He became quite enraged at that thought, just as he was when defending his position earlier. Generally speaking, he appeared to me at times – even in his appearance – much more manly, more self-

Left, poster advertising four concerts given by the Society for Private Musical Performances in May and June 1919, to which guests were 'exceptionally' invited so that the Society's aims could be more widely made known.

Above, Webern and Berg photographed together near Klagenfurt, c. 1920

confident, more unyielding, harder.' The situation was further
enlivened by the decision of Mathilde Schoenberg and Wilhelmine,
who had evidently never much liked each other, to fall out as well;
when some food supplies earlier requested by Schoenberg arrived via
Wilhelmine's aunt in Mürzzuschlag, Mathilde returned them. Given
the meagre rations to which everyone had been reduced after four
years of war, this amounted to a calculated and mortal insult.
Webern decided to move to the Carinthian village of Ettendorf a
few kilometres east of Schwabegg and the Preglhof, well away from
Schoenberg (and Mathilde).

He had got as far as arranging for his belongings to be sent there
when Schoenberg, realizing that Webern was too important to his
plans for the Society for Private Musical Performances to be allowed
to disappear into the Lower Carinthian countryside, offered an olive
branch in the form of a brusquely conciliatory letter. ('I have not
many friends, it is true, but the few I have can rely on me entirely.')
The breach was duly healed with what experienced Webern-watchers

The proclamation of the
First Austrian Republic on
the steps of the Parliament
building, Vienna,
12 November 1918

Aftermath of the war:
gathering firewood in the
Vienna Woods, 1919

Campaign poster preceding
the Carinthian plebiscite,
October 1920, regarding
Yugoslavia's claim on part
of the province's territory.
The inscription reads 'Your
Heimat calls you!' and
'Stay loyal to Carinthia!'

must have recognized as suspicious ease, and the society was
inaugurated in late November. A fortnight earlier the German army's
failure to break through on the western front after four years of
trench warfare had at last brought about the capitulation of the
central powers and the end of the war. Germany signed an
armistice on 11 November; Austria–Hungary had surrendered a
week previously.

Peacetime brought no easing of the desperate shortages in and
around Vienna, but the grim conditions did not prevent the
Schoenberg circle from proceeding with their new project. Webern
and his colleagues were kept busy with a schedule that encompassed
twenty-six concerts during the opening 1918–19 season, during which
Schoenberg, adamant that the society should not be seen as a personal
musical fiefdom, would not permit any of his own works to be
played, and also programmed only a few by Webern and Berg. The
society's polyglot repertory ranged from Pfitzner, Webern's erstwhile
not-quite-teacher, to England's Frederick Delius, France's Darius
Milhaud and Paul Dukas, Italy's Alfredo Casella, the Moravian-Czech
Leoš Janáček (who, though a world figure today, was then almost
unknown other than locally), and some thirty other composers. A
strong initial response by the society's membership meant that its
concerts soon moved from the Schwarzwald School to the small halls
of Vienna's Konzerthaus and Musikverein. Its activities were limited

by the relatively small amount of high-quality talent that was prepared to perform under its auspices for a negligible fee, but some superb musicians were nonetheless attracted by the seriousness of the enterprise. Notable among these was a young Polish–Jewish pianist, Eduard Steuermann, then twenty-six years old, who took part in the main offering of the inaugural concert: a performance of a piano-duet version of Mahler's Seventh Symphony, for which Schoenberg coached the two players for a staggering total of twelve rehearsals lasting four hours each.

In the wake of the central powers' defeat, the Habsburg Empire now disintegrated. The emperor, Franz Joseph, had died in 1916 at the age of eighty-six, and the demise of Austria–Hungary was accelerated by the terms of the peace treaty drawn up by the Allies. Austria was made to cede huge tracts of territory to the newly created states of Yugoslavia, Czechoslovakia (which had provided most of the empire's coal production and heavy industry) and Hungary (which had provided most of its food), and also to Poland and Romania. Most contentiously of all for the German-speaking populations that lived there, South Tyrol and the peninsula of Istria on the Adriatic were both ceded to Italy. The small remaining area that now made up the Republic of Austria was insufficient for the country immediately to feed itself; its industrial base was similarly inadequate; and a third of the entire population lived in the capital, Vienna. The patriotic euphoria that had so intoxicated Webern and millions of his compatriots in August 1914 must have felt much more than four years distant as the new, truncated, demographically unbalanced republic set about trying to establish itself in a hostile peacetime world.

It was some time, too, before the last of the fighting actually stopped. Carinthia, an area of mixed Slovene and German-speaking population, was invaded by Yugoslav troops who occupied Klagenfurt in May 1919, with resistance in the surrounding countryside coming from armed local militias calling themselves the Heimwehr, or Home Guard. A plebiscite held under the auspices of Italy (which had an interest in restricting the territorial growth of neighbouring Yugoslavia) established that the majority of the local population wished to remain part of Austria. But the success of the armed Heimwehr – later significantly to be known also as the Heimatschutz (*Heimat* Protection League) – in proving an effective influence over political procedure had set a disturbing precedent for the future of the First Austrian Republic. Webern meanwhile must have been outraged to discover that as a result of this protracted exercise in map-drawing, the Hochstuhl, his beloved mountain to the south of Klagenfurt, had ended up on the wrong side of the Yugoslav border.

Two main political parties had evolved in Austria during the nineteenth century: the left-of-centre Social Democrats, and the Christian Socials, whose programme was a peculiar Austrian blend of populist, nationalist, monarchist and Catholic elements. The Social Democrats, finding themselves in a majority in the new state assembly's coalition government immediately after the war, drew up a republican constitution reflecting their own influence. Since its beginnings the party had always been more than a parliamentary vote-chaser; concerts, theatrical events, expeditions to the countryside, educational classes, and the foundation of choral groups all took place under its auspices, as a way of earning its working-class members' political loyalty. This sense of social responsibility could be traced back to the eighteenth century, when the ideals of the Age of Enlightenment had influenced the early versions of similar policies enacted (despite entrenched feudal opposition) by the Habsburg Empress Maria Theresa and by her son and successor, Joseph II. The Social Democrats' updated equivalent was soon to be of major importance to Webern's career.

There was little the new Austrian government could do immediately, however, to relieve its citizens' widespread hardship. The advent of summer, always much cherished by Webern, was more welcome than ever in 1919; at least he and his family, like millions of others, could now keep warm. They holidayed as usual in Mürzzuschlag, where Webern punctuated a fruitful period of composing with an ascent of the nearby and spectacular Hochschwab – an experience about which he wrote to Berg, who was evidently a willing listener to his friend's ideas.

Following page, the summit of the Hochschwab in Styria, which Webern frequently climbed in the 1920s

It was glorious, because this is not sport for me, not amusement, but something quite different: it is a search for the highest, a discovery of correspondences in nature for everything that serves me as a model, a model for all that I would like to have within myself … These high ravines with their mountain pines and mysterious plants. The latter, above

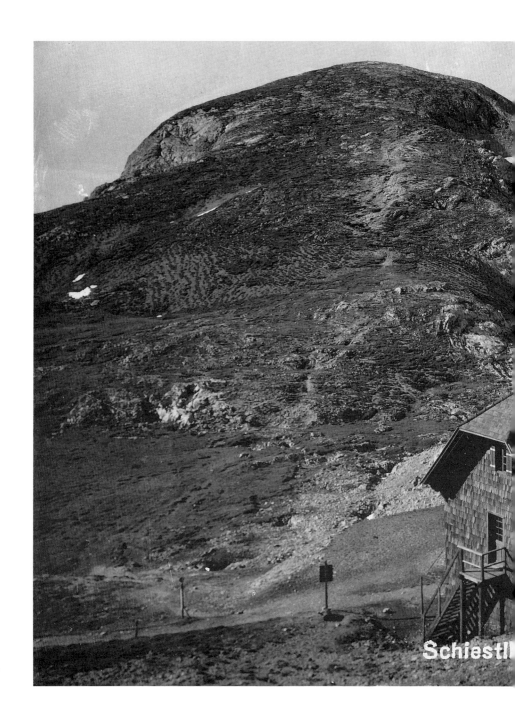

160 m mit Hochschwabgipfel, 2278 m.

all, touch me deeply. But not because they are so 'beautiful'. It is not the beautiful landscape, the beautiful flowers in the usual romantic sense, that move me. My objective is the deep, unfathomable, inexhaustible meaning in everything, especially in these manifestations of nature. All nature is dear to me, but that which expresses itself 'up there' is the dearest of all. I want to progress … in the purely physical knowledge of all these phenomena. That is why I always carry my botanical lexicon with me … This physical reality contains all the miracles.

The music Webern had been composing intermittently over the past five years now began to assemble into a sequence of song-cycles whose evolution cannot be traced in chronological order: Webern set each individual song without at first having a definite idea as to the final shape of the work to which it would contribute. That shape was eventually decided as much by the settings' instrumentation as by the connections, or otherwise, between the poems themselves. By the end of July 1919 Webern had in this way completed the Four Songs Op. 12 for voice and piano, the Four Songs Op. 13 for voice and chamber orchestra, and all but one of the Six Songs on poems of Georg Trakl for voice, clarinet, bass clarinet, violin, and cello (the last song would follow two years later). He also produced an almost equal number of unpublished settings, some complete and some only sketched, some using poems by the same writers and some not. There are also a few unpublished movements for string quartet which disprove the long-assumed notion that at this period, Webern was writing *only* vocal works.

The fact that songs so dominated his musical thinking during these years, however, does indicate something about Webern's consuming love of composing for the voice. It is possible that this preoccupation related to an artistic need to break free of the extreme fragmentation and compression of his instrumental works of the preceding years, a need answered up to a point by the necessarily longer musical lines involved in word-setting. But there is no evidence that Webern felt that music as impacted as that of the Six Bagatelles or the Three Pieces for Cello and Piano amounted to any kind of creative cul-de-sac. It is rather that, surrounded by difficult wartime conditions and even more difficult peacetime ones, he turned to the voice – the purest of instruments – as a central, life-giving source which he had consciously begun to treasure as representing the essence of music itself.

Whatever the precise creative impulse at their heart, this first group of middle-period songs shows that artistically at least, the advent of the war had been good for Webern. Much of this music has a fresh-air, out-of-doors quality quite different from the feverish sophistication of many of the preceding works, indicating that the experience of getting away both from Schoenberg and from the stresses and strains of artistic life in Vienna had propelled Webern's creativity into new and vivid musical territory. The introverted mood associated with his broodings on the death of his mother, too, is from now on strikingly absent. The best of the Four Songs Op. 12 recapture the note of guileless simplicity which is a Webernian trademark, and which ever since his earliest songs had rather receded in the face of the headlong stylistic adventures of recent years. Its return here coincides, in the enchanting first song of the opus 12 set, with a new development. This is Webern's first song on a sacred text: not a liturgical one, but an anonymous hymn to the Virgin Mary in a folksong-like style to which Webern was from now on increasingly to be drawn. Like many people in wartime, he seems to have discovered a need for a religious response to terrestrial existence, although he was never to be a regular church-goer.

The Four Songs Op. 13 with chamber orchestra relate more directly to the musical territory of his immediately pre-war works (the second song was in fact written early in 1914) although here, too, the rarefied Expressionism of that period is transformed into a cooler, purer musical diction indicative of the later Webern. But it is in the Trakl Songs that the most radical development takes place. Webern responded to the German poet's disturbed, landscape-suffused imagery with settings whose musical idiom is denser than anything he had attempted before. The songs' marvellously supple and expressive vocal lines interweave with intricately wrought accompaniments whose austere instrumentation leads the ear to concentrate on their purely musical workings, rather than on the technical firework-display that the use of an orchestra might have induced. (Several of Webern's other unfinished Trakl settings at this time were planned for orchestra, but he remained dissatisfied with them.)

Another feature of the Trakl Songs is the advanced nature of their writing for the voice. In performance this demands a combination of immaculate technical control with a lyrical style of delivery very different from the dramatic convulsions explored a few years earlier by Schoenberg in his monodrama *Erwartung* ('Expectation'), or from the speech-like declamation of his *Pierrot Lunaire* cycle. It takes a specially gifted singer to do justice on every level to Webern's song-settings from the Trakl Songs onwards; given their musical riches, however, the rewards are disproportionately great. (Eduard Steuermann once expressed doubt about the feasibility of some of Webern's more extreme demands on the human voice. Webern replied: 'Don't worry; we feel and write, they will find a way.')

The summer's composing in Mürzzuschlag in 1919 came to an abrupt halt in August when Carl von Webern was taken ill in Klagenfurt. Webern hurried there to find that the Yugoslav occupation of the city had only just ended, and that the experience of this after the events of the preceding years had been too much for his father, who died a few days later. A saddened Webern stayed for the burial at the cemetery at Annabichl on the outskirts of the town, and then returned to Mürzzuschlag to take the family back to Vienna. The forthcoming winter was dominated by his ceaseless work for the Society for Private Musical Performances, by the ever-persisting shortages of food and coal, and by the arrival of another daughter, Christine, who was born in November. The family's difficulties became so great that Webern sent the three oldest children to stay with relatives while Wilhelmine tried somehow to keep the baby warmer and less hungry than she and her husband were. Eventually they abandoned the Mödling apartment and stayed with the Mörtl family in Vienna until the spring. The ensuing months brought further events and developments: another holiday in Mürzzuschlag; the publication by Universal Edition in Vienna of four of Webern's works (a long-promised project delayed by the war, and representing the start of Webern's permanent association with the company); and two very successful performances of Schoenberg's *Gurrelieder* at the Vienna State Opera, conducted by the composer, for which Webern coached the 400-strong Schubertbund chorus.

An additional disaster to those which Austria had inflicted on herself in the preceding years was the hyperinflation that now destroyed the currency, the Krone (crown). The problem, incipient since the end of the war, had been worsened by the government's ruinous decision to print money as a hoped-for way out of the crisis, so that by 1922 the Krone was almost valueless. Webern's Preglhof inheritance, on which he and Wilhelmine had been existing for years while Webern lived only for Art, was wiped out. The result in the country as a whole, as in similarly inflation-decimated Germany, was a deepening spiral of economic collapse, mass unemployment, demonstrations, and riots: a situation which over the next few years began to transform the existing mood of resentment at the Allied powers' punitive peace terms into an underlying desire for revenge. The refusal of France in particular to contemplate any post-war territorial gains by Germany ruled out any possibility of Austrian and German unification, which many Austrians believed would help their crippled economy back to its feet, for all the historical differences between the two countries. The general situation was also a perfect breeding-ground for pan-German feeling of a more sinister kind. The First Republic's built-in political instability became alarmingly clear from the results of two regional plebiscites held in 1921 on the question of unification. In Tyrol, 98·6 per cent of the votes cast were in favour; in the province of Salzburg, the figure was 99·3 per cent.

The Society for Private Musical Performances, despite the loyal support it attracted from its small but enthusiastic membership of around 300, fell victim to the currency collapse in 1922. By then,

Banknote in the new Austrian currency, the Schilling, January 1924, equivalent to 10,000 Kronen

however, Webern's professional life was at last beginning to find a firm footing. The Schubertbund chorus, much impressed by his work with them for their *Gurrelieder* performances in 1920, asked him to take over as their conductor for their 1921–2 concert season. This was highly successful, and although the arrangement was terminated after only five months – Webern's rehearsal methods having been deemed too intensive for the sizeable contingent of the membership that preferred an easy-going night out – word had quickly got around that here was a choral conductor of great quality. As a result Webern began a long and fruitful association with his local Mödlinger Männer-gesangverein (the Mödling Male Voice Choir, also incorporating a women's chorus), whose conductor he became in late 1921. Another significant invitation came early in 1922. The Social Democratic Party had since 1905 sponsored a series of Workers Symphony Concerts as part of its programme of bringing art to the working population. Although the party had recently lost power nationally to the Christian Socials, it continued to govern the city of Vienna, and had recently established a Kunststelle (arts council) to oversee its cultural programme. Early in 1922 Webern was invited by David Josef Bach, who ran the Workers Symphony Concerts series in Vienna, to conduct two performances of Mahler's Third Symphony in the large hall of the Konzerthaus.

Both evenings were a sensation. After the first performance Berg wrote to his wife: 'After the first and last movements, I felt exactly as one would after an adrenalin injection. I could not stand up.' Two days later Schoenberg and his wife were also present. 'I sat with Schoenberg,' Berg wrote to Helene. 'He had not thought it possible. Webern's achievement is such that it can only be compared with that of Mahler himself, and such that all doubts [about his ability], even those of Mathilde, were swept away to be replaced by unreserved admiration.' The triumvirate of Schoenberg, Webern and Berg was admittedly something of a mutual admiration society: an under-standable situation, given the hostility that their music had almost always encountered outside a friendly circle of supporters. Even so, neutral reports of the two concerts indicate that the performances were indeed remarkable. With his ill-fated attempt at a career in opera finally out of the way, Webern's conducting skills had now flowered wonderfully in the concert-hall.

These events, along with the publication of some of his music, initiated for him a career as a composer–conductor which during the next few years was at last to bring him a measure of public success, internationally as well as locally. His conducting methods met with the same response as his approach to choral rehearsals: opinion among orchestral players was sharply divided between those who found Webern impossibly pedagogic, analytical and punctilious, and those who were won over by his dedicated musicianship to a position of respect and, not infrequently, deep admiration. Needless to say, with Webern's fierce pride as an artist involved, there were occasional thunderstorms. Later in 1922 he was rehearsing the Vienna Konzert-verein orchestra for the latest of a sequence of so far extremely successful concerts when, as he wrote to Heinrich Jalowetz, his painstaking exposition of a musical point to the violin section became too much for one of the other players.

At the Donaueschingen Festival, July 1924: (from left) the composer and conductor Otto Klemperer, Schoenberg, Webern, and the conductor Hermann Scherchen

At this point, the first trombonist rose and gave a speech telling me that I was wrong, I was not *in a* music school, *I was insulting the orchestra with every word, that this was no way to rehearse, and that I should go to a movie house in order to acquire the necessary routine for myself ... I answered the speech of the trombonist quite calmly and objectively and conducted the rehearsal to the end (the incident was right at the beginning).* Rehearsing proceeded with the *greatest of* attention *and in* deadly silence. *Probably they had noticed how deeply hurt I was. During intermission a deputation from the orchestra (among them the trombonist) came and tried to conciliate and to* apologize. *But my decision had been made: after consultation with Schoenberg, I telegraphed the Konzertverein that, because of this incident, I would not conduct the orchestra any more and that I was cancelling the concerts (including the coming one).*

Webern and David Josef Bach (front row, first – with hands clasped – and second from left) with members of the Singverein chorus at Mahler's grave in Grinzing cemetery, Vienna, 18 May 1926

It must be emphasized, however, that such peremptory behaviour on Webern's part was not typical at this time. News gradually travelled around the post-war European musical scene that here was a conductor seriously worth engaging if the orchestra in question was

likely to be able to handle his meticulous rehearsal methods; and compared to his former instability when dealing with the workings of an opera company, Webern's now absolute need to earn a regular living helped to keep his volatile artistic idealism on a much more even keel. To begin with this new career did not earn enough to make much difference to his dire financial situation. Wilhelmine took up knitting to bring in what little money she could; Webern sold some of the choicest volumes in his cherished library of books and musical scores; and Schoenberg, reciprocating the support that Webern had so often shown him in similar circumstances, successfully appealed to various patrons more than once to make a donation to the hard-pressed father of four. Very gradually Webern's financial position began to stabilize in parallel with that of Austria herself, as the Christian Social government headed by Ignaz Seipel secured sufficient foreign loans to bring the inflationary slide to a halt and eventually to introduce a new currency, the Schilling.

Alongside his new conducting career, Webern's music now started to become known outside Vienna; the Passacaglia especially began to meet with a much warmer response than it had at its 1908 première, notably when Zemlinsky conducted it in Prague in 1922. Other works, however, continued to be less well received. An eye-witness report of a performance of the Five Movements for String Quartet in Salzburg the same year describes an occasion resembling, if on a smaller scale, the legendary 'Battle of the Musikverein' of 1913. The two vocal participants were, naturally, Viennese: the composer Wilhelm Grosz and the architect Adolf Loos, a noted supporter of the Schoenberg school.

It was during the quiet fourth movement that a loud outcry 'furchtbar!' [terrible] was heard. It was Herr Grosz objecting to the new music. From the other aisle came the equally forceful 'Maulhalten!' [Shut up]. Grosz insisted that he had paid for his ticket and was entitled to his opinion, whereupon both men rose and went for each other. Half the audience got up and took an active part in the mêlée. The quartet had fled by this time and police rushed in from all sides … Anton von Webern

*appeared atop the orchestra staircase, listening to the overpowering bravos
of the progressives and all those who were horrified by the inexcusable
incident. The battle of applause lasted at least ten minutes, when it was
announced from the stage that the programme would not continue.
Anyway, the hall had been ordered cleared by the guardians of the law …
Next day some fifty musicians were invited to hear the quartet in its
entirety in a special performance.*

But the reaction to Webern's more 'difficult' music was by no
means always so hostile. In 1924, at the contemporary-music festival
held every summer at Prinz Egon Fürstenberg's castle in the town of
Donaueschingen in southwestern Germany, Webern conducted the
première of his Trakl Songs, and a quartet led by the violinist Rudolf
Kolisch gave the first performance of the Six Bagatelles. The response
in the musical press was startled, but generally favourable. 'A kind of
musical Beardsley', wrote one critic, not altogether unperceptively in
respect of the Bagatelles at least. Another wrote of these pieces that
they possessed 'a concentration of musical thinking, a conciseness of
expression that convinced even the unprepared listener of the spirituality of this introvert musician'. Webern must have been pleased to
read this even if, as he reported to Berg, he had been less pleased by
a momentary hitch in the performance itself. 'After the first two
movements there was laughter. I then considered not conducting my
songs. Finally calm. The songs went excellently.'

The family's summer holidays, apart from a stay with the
Schoenbergs at Traunkirchen in the Salzkammergut in 1922, were
spent mostly in and around Afflenz, a little village near Mürzzuschlag.
Above it rose the slopes and precipices of what had become Webern's
favourite mountain, the Hochschwab, which he climbed repeatedly
from the Bürgeralm, a hut situated on the tree line high above the
village. In previous years the demands made by Webern's growing
family might have frustrated his traditional summer-holiday urge to
create, but he had by now found that he could usually compose
satisfactorily at home in his Mödling apartment, despite the disrup-
tion caused by his conducting engagements and by his need to
supplement his income by taking on private pupils. By the autumn
of 1926 he had in this way assembled a further five collections of
songs to add to their post-war predecessors.

Again the chronology of the individual published items, as of their
unpublished satellites, overlaps intricately; and the accompaniments
of each set, like those of the Trakl Songs, are for various small
instrumental combinations without piano. The Five Sacred Songs
combine the open-air spirituality of the first of the Four Songs Op. 12
with a further development of the musical density of the Trakl Songs,
to rare and austerely beautiful effect (although, again, it takes a
superlative level of performance to convey the compositional mastery,
at once brilliant and serene, that lies behind the music's formidable
surface difficulties). The Five Canons each set a Latin text from the
Catholic liturgy, apart from the second which, like the second of the
Five Sacred Songs, comes from *Des Knaben Wunderhorn* ('The Youth's
Magic Horn'), the nineteenth-century anthology of folk-poetry from
which Mahler had taken many of his song-texts. Webern's Five
Canons recast the technical procedures of his revered Netherlands
choral composers in a new, winsomely unpretentious, flawlessly
masterful way. (Also dating from 1924 is a small piano piece entitled
Kinderstück – 'Children's Piece' – whose artless simplicity of manner
conceals its significance as the first music by Webern consciously
to make use of Schoenberg's recently evolved twelve-note technique.
Since, however, the device did not at this stage radically influence
the style of Webern's music, discussion of it is deferred until the
following chapter.)

The Three Traditional Rhymes, based on anonymous German
folk-songs, and the Three Songs Op. 18, which set a selection of
material similar to that of the preceding cycles, push Webern's
musical discoveries of recent years to unprecedented extremes of
angularity and difficulty; it is questionable whether an entirely
commanding and accurate performance by any singer of the opus 18
settings is actually feasible. There is a strong sense in this work that
Webern was pursuing a genre of musical transcendence that is simply
beyond the capacity of a small line-up of vocal and instrumental
forces. As if digesting the mixed success of such a bold experiment,
the Two Songs on texts by Goethe that Webern set for mixed chorus
and small chamber group in the summer of 1926 are markedly and
attractively simpler in style.

His life, like his work, was going its own way. Schoenberg, whose
wife Mathilde had died in 1923, had the following year married

Gertrude Kolisch – sister of the violinist Rudolf Kolisch – and was now teaching composition in a prestigious post at the Prussian Academy of Arts in Berlin. Alban Berg had leapt to international fame with the première of his first opera, *Wozzeck*, also in Berlin in 1925. Meanwhile Webern continued his austere life of composing and private teaching in Mödling, supplementing his slim earnings by also teaching piano and choral singing at Vienna's Israelitic Institute for the Blind, and emerging every so often from this routine to conduct a series of concerts which steadily enhanced his reputation. The most memorable of these were the performances of Mahler's huge choral and orchestral Eighth Symphony (the so-called 'Symphony of a Thousand') which, after weeks of meticulous preparation, Webern conducted in the Konzerthaus to celebrate the twentieth anniversary of the Workers Symphony Concerts. Both occasions were an overwhelming triumph, the greatest he ever had as a conductor. As one review put it: 'With this performance of the Eighth, Anton Webern would have become a famous conductor elsewhere, but in Vienna …'

Yet in a sense his heart was not on the conductor's rostrum, under the spotlight of attention, glamour, and potential fame; it had found its true territory in quite different regions. In July 1923 Webern had written to Schoenberg after a summer break with his family in Afflenz, his ex-teacher having recently secured for him one of the donations that were helping to tide over his then impoverished finances.

Perhaps you found it frivolous that I dared, in such uncertain times, to undertake a tour of several days with my family … my wife was entirely against the idea. But I wanted to give her and the children a little pleasure; therefore I did not give in to her … It is impossible to describe what a beneficial influence the stay at such height has had upon all of us. Without exaggeration: the purest physical rebirth … I carried Christl across snow fields, in an icy mountain storm, almost to the summit of the Hochschwab. In a shepherd's hut we warmed our frozen limbs by the fire. Never before has it seemed to me as beautiful 'up there' as this time with my family.

5

Traunkirchen on the
Traunsee, where Webern
visited Schoenberg in
August 1921 and stayed
for seven weeks with his
own family during the
summer of 1922

*I want to understand in order the better to
feel, to feel in order the better to understand.
I want to be truly classical, and to rediscover
the classical approach through nature
and sensation.*

Paul Cézanne

Through the Looking-Glass 1926–34

The scene is the green, mountain-fringed countryside near the village of Traunkirchen on the Traunsee in the Salzkammergut. The date is July 1921. Schoenberg, who is on holiday with his family at a villa by the lake, is out walking with Josef Rufer, one of his current generation of pupils. He turns to Rufer and says (or is reported to have said): 'Today I have discovered something which will ensure the supremacy of German music for the next hundred years.'

This is the first recorded statement made by Schoenberg regarding the twelve-note technique – the method of musical composition which has ever since been the subject of vast quantities of polemical barricade-building and disinformation, encompassing every shade of ideological opinion from fanatical support to implacable hostility. For many would-be listeners the whole idea has duly come to resemble a dark, uninviting cavern presided over by a lurking dragon called Schoenberg, and fronted by a sign reading 'Mathematical Music'. The concept of twelve-note music – also known as serialism or 'twelve-tone' music (a mistranslation of the German word *zwölfton*) – can

Webern by the piano at which he composed in his home in Mödling, summer 1930

indeed seem bewildering at a first encounter. But for anyone prepared to disregard as much as possible of the avalanche of nonsense that has been said and written about it since July 1921, it is nowhere near as impenetrable as legend would suggest. Besides, the influences and impulses behind its evolution constitute much of the story told in the preceding chapters.

So what is this twelve-note technique exactly? Contrary to myth, the basic principle is simple enough.

Ever since Schoenberg's and Webern's discovery of what appeared to be a new musical sound-world of freely chromatic, so-called 'atonal' harmony early in 1909, their instinct had been to press on ever deeper into this unexplored territory. But to compose music requires technical articulation as well as instinctive inspiration. It soon became clear that the time-honoured codification of the traditional 'tonal' harmony of Western classical music – the musical grammar that had served the differing needs of Mozart, Beethoven, Brahms, and company – no longer applied directly to the syntax of post-1909 total chromaticism. The so-called twelve-note 'law' – a term deployed by Schoenberg in the sense that gravity, for instance, is a naturally occurring law, as distinct from an arbitrarily enforceable rule – therefore evolved as a possible means of rationalizing the new situation.

It is an acoustical phenomenon of totally chromatic music that, as a composer states a given number of individual notes from among the twelve that make up the Western chromatic scale – whether those notes are stated as a unit of melody, or as a chord, or as a combination of both – the effect is to create a harmonic gap which the remaining, hitherto unstated notes are duly drawn to fill. Depending on the context the effect can be as powerful, in musical terms, as the force with which opposite magnetic poles attract.

Accordingly the essence of Schoenberg's twelve-note law is that the entire melodic and harmonic substance of a musical composition has as its source a row (or series) of *all twelve* notes of the Western scale – in this way satisfying the aural desire for the balancing of these self-contained harmonic forces – and that the twelve notes of this row occur throughout the composition *in a chosen and unchanging order*. (Too restricting? Not really. The composer can choose from a possible 479,001,600 twelve-note combinations.) Each statement of the row is

worked through fully before the next begins; and each can begin on
any of the individual notes of the scale, since this does not alter the
row's content, but only its relative altitude (much as a major or minor
key in traditional tonality is instantly discernible as such, whether
higher or lower in pitch).

The row can also be stated either in its basic form, or upside down
('inversion'), or backwards ('retrograde'), or both backwards and
upside down at once ('retrograde inversion'). Schoenberg once
likened this procedure to looking at a hat from different angles:
whether viewed upside down or the right way up or sideways or end-
ways on, it is always recognizable as the same hat. (In a lecture given
in 1932 Webern used the same illustrative device, this time substi-
tuting the hat with an ashtray.) Schoenberg's simile of course ignores
the ridiculously obvious fact that a hat is a hat and music is music;
one is perceived visually, the other aurally, and the difference is
absolute. Besides, the technical device of inverting or reversing a
melodic line or lines had been a stock-in-trade of contrapuntal
composition for centuries; Bach often used it, as did the Netherlands
Renaissance masters. Schoenberg's capacity for top-heavy irony
should never be underestimated. It is entirely possible that the much-
quoted 'hat' analogy was a miscued Schoenbergian joke which failed
to be seen as such at the time, and which has been taken with
mournful seriousness ever since.

The same judicious scepticism needs to be applied to Schoenberg's
reported remark to Rufer regarding the 'supremacy of German music
for the next hundred years' – an odd statement from an Austrian Jew,
at least if taken at face value. But was it meant to be so taken? Or was
it yet another advanced exercise in Schoenbergian irony? Schoenberg
was only in Traunkirchen at all because his summer holiday, which he
had begun a few weeks earlier in the village of Mattsee on the nearby
Obertrumersee, had been interrupted in the unsavoury style that
was becoming typical of the times; Jews, he had been informed by a
deputation of local dignitaries, were no longer welcome in Mattsee.
In the circumstances it is hard to envisage Schoenberg being
sympathetic to ideas of 'German supremacy' of any kind. On the
other hand he never wavered in his belief in the absolute centrality of
the Austro-German tradition in Western music. Given that the exact
context of his remark in the conversation with Rufer is not known,

the remark itself – if it is indeed exactly what Schoenberg said – remains a conundrum.

Further qualifications regarding the supposed dogmatism of Schoenberg's 'law' can usefully be made. First, there is no such thing as a single twelve-note 'system', neither in Schoenberg's music, nor in Webern's, nor in anyone else's. It is significant that Schoenberg, who wrote a number of textbooks on musical subjects – harmony, counterpoint, form, fundamentals of composition – never wrote one on twelve-note technique, and never taught it to any of his pupils. (Neither did Webern.) There exists a potentially infinite variety of twelve-note methods; Webern, like Schoenberg, used more than one approach at various times, as has virtually every other twelve-note composer since. Some even had earlier. The Austrian composer Josef Matthias Hauer, a younger contemporary of Schoenberg, had developed independently and at roughly the same time his own, differently functioning twelve-note method, a situation which later led to a rather silly series of public claims and counter-claims as to who had 'got there first'. (Schoenberg nonetheless had some of Hauer's music played at the Society for Private Musical Performances.) In the early years of the twentieth century the American composer Charles Ives, working in near-total isolation from the European classical tradition, arrived at an idiosyncratic prototype of twelve-note composition in the course of his own heady voyage of musical dis-covery (although, unlike Schoenberg, Ives did not develop the idea into a central strand of compositional practice).

The description 'serial', too, is often used as if it were inter-changeable with 'twelve-note'. This is a little misleading, since the deployment of a given order of notes 'in series' does not auto-matically presuppose that all twelve notes of the chromatic scale are involved. Strict counterpoint, particularly canonic counterpoint, amounts to a genre of serial procedure; it can be argued that many passages in Bach or Josquin des Près, for instance, are in this sense 'serial music'. Technically it is correct to describe Webern's twelve-note works up to and including his String Trio of 1927 – with the occasional rare exception, such as the third of the Three Songs Op. 18 – as twelve-note only, and those that followed as combining both twelve-note and serial methods to varying extents. For simplicity's sake, the term 'twelve-note' will from here onwards be used to encompass both categories.

Following page, one of Webern's favourite mountains: the Dachstein (2,995 metres), fifty-five kilometres southeast of Salzburg, viewed westwards towards the Bavarian Alps on the horizon

Several points, then, cannot be emphasized too strongly. There are at least as many twelve-note methods as there are composers who use them. There exists convincing or unconvincing twelve-note music written by talented or talentless composers as with any other kind of music. And since composing or analysing twelve-note music requires numerical skills no more formidable than being able to count from one to twelve, the description 'mathematical music' is both meaningless and absurd. Indeed it can be submitted that the technique and cast of mind underpinning much of Bach's music is more 'mathematical' than anything in Webern (let alone in Schoenberg).

The development of Webern's music in the years immediately after the First World War had encompassed a gradual approach towards a fairly elementary twelve-note method, a process which may or may not have been influenced by unrecorded discussions with Schoenberg on the subject. Then, in February 1923, Schoenberg summoned some chosen members of his circle to his house in Mödling so that they could spend the morning listening to him officially unveil the new technique, which he illustrated with the prelude of his recently composed Piano Suite. Webern was present, as was Eduard Steuermann, who remembered Webern saying on the way home: 'That's it! I always had the feeling that when I introduced the twelfth note, the piece had ended.' With the advantage of hindsight, the extreme chromatic penetration in Webern's pre-war music from 1909 onwards does indeed seem to hint at the early stages of twelve-note procedure. Embryonic traces of the technique in the middle-period songs, with their greater density of musical activity, are harder to discern unmistakably. The sketches for the fourth of the Five Sacred Songs, however, include a fully written-out twelve-note row, together with its inverted and retrograde versions. The song was composed in July 1922, while Webern was on holiday at Traunkirchen, with Schoenberg nearby.

The first work in which Webern appears consciously to have used the twelve-note method throughout is a little *Kinderstück* ('Children's Piece') for piano, composed at Mödling in the autumn of 1924, and using the relatively conventional rhythmic language to which Schoenberg had largely (though not exclusively) reverted in his own early twelve-note works written at this time. The effect in Webern's

piece, however, is of a deliberately cultivated spareness and simplicity
reminiscent of some of the Four Songs Op. 12 and the Five Canons:
a style wholly personal to him, and quite different from the knowing
sophistication with which Schoenberg explored existing Classical
and dance forms in his music of the early 1920s. Webern's Three
Traditional Rhymes, Three Songs Op. 18, and Two Songs on texts by
Goethe – all written between 1924 and 1926 – variously develop, in
parallel with the complex technical legacy of his pre-war Expressionist
works, this instinct for simplicity of musical diction. The slightly
earlier Five Canons – whose construction is not strictly twelve-note –
had shown Webern's continuing preoccupation with another, similarly
radical technique of musical rationalization: Netherlands-inspired
strict counterpoint.

Now, in the autumn of 1926, encouraged by his growing confidence in handling the twelve-note idea, Webern felt able to embark
on his first non-vocal work for thirteen years which is other than a
fragment: his String Trio. This reached its final form, in mid-1927,
of two quite large movements (by Webernian standards), having
engendered the creation of a number of satellite movements and
fragments along the way. Structurally, the Trio relates to Classical
forms: the first, slowish movement is a rondo, the second, faster one
a sonata-form movement with a slow introduction. Musically, for all
its ceaseless richness of invention, this is perhaps Webern's most
demanding work for an audience. The players have to deliver a
stylish rendition of Webern's steeply geared middle-period idiom at
its most intricate. Yet this very intricacy effectively masks the structural course of the music for any listener who is not graced with the
acutest ear and memory, or who does not happen to have a copy of
the score helpfully to hand.

Had Webern taken this line of stylistic development much further,
the outcome might have been a genre of musical foliage so dense as to
be virtually impenetrable. Whether or not he consciously realized this,
he was soon working on a new instrumental composition in which his
musical style was to emerge transformed. The new work's completion
is mentioned in the course of a letter he wrote in June 1928 to the
poetess whose writings were to be the central inspiration of his later
life (along with the creative possibilities opened up by the twelve-note
row itself).

Webern had first met Hildegard Jone in 1926. The daughter of an Austrian architect, she was married to Josef Humplik, one of the leading sculptors of the radically minded 'Vienna Secession' group of artists who in the early years of the century had rebelled against the city's prevailing artistic conservatism. Hildegard Jone had at first trained as a sculptor at the Vienna Academy under Humplik's tuition; after their marriage she turned increasingly to painting and poetry, producing much in both media but exhibiting and publishing little. From this time on, all of Webern's vocal works were to use texts only by Jone, so complete was the affinity that he sensed between the metaphysical, nature-suffused spirituality of her poetry and that of his own music.

A self-portrait by Hildegard Jone, whose poetry inspired all of Webern's later vocal works

His published letters to the Humpliks give a likeable picture of
the affectionate closeness of the two couples; the general tone is
relaxed, spontaneous, and quite different from the earnest self-
justification that tended to dominate Webern's correspondence with
Schoenberg. Wilhelmine, too, evidently liked the Humpliks as much
as her husband did, to judge from the references to 'we' which
constantly recur whenever thanks are offered for hospitality shared
and gifts exchanged. More than any other Webern-related documents, the letters to the Humpliks give unpretentious voice to the
ideas that lay at the heart of the serene creativity of Webern's last
years – a creativity that was to remain miraculously immune to the
appalling terrestrial events which before long were to engulf the lives
of both couples.

In August 1928 Webern wrote to Hildegard Jone, quoting some of
her own words:

> *I understand the word 'Art' as meaning the faculty of presenting a
> thought in the clearest, simplest form, that is, the most 'graspable' form …
> And that's why I have never understood the meaning of 'classical',
> 'romantic', and the rest, and I have never placed myself in opposition to
> the masters of the past but have always tried to do just like them: to say
> what it is given to me to say with the utmost clarity … And so then I am
> also entirely of your opinion when you say: 'We must come to believe that
> the only road onward is inwards.' Yes: 'Every heart colours differently its
> evening, when it sets.' …*
>
> *The work of which I have already spoken to you – a 'Symphony' in
> two movements – is finished.*

As with the String Trio, the Symphony's final two-movement form
had only been reached after much trial and error. Again, Classical
forms are the structural model: the slow first movement is in sonata
form, while the quicker and much shorter second is a set of
variations. The music's most striking feature is the measured diction
which dominates all of the first movement and much of the second.
Compared to the String Trio's torrent of sonically iridescent, rhythmically complex, post-Expressionist hyperactivity, the Symphony
stakes out a totally new sound-world: distilled, austere, rhythmically
much simpler, with the music's expressivity now essentially internal,

and with abundant listener-friendly fresh air around the individual notes. Technically, what has taken place is an intersection of the twelve-note method with the canonic devices of Netherlands Renaissance polyphony, whose sculpted purity of utterance now steps decisively to the foreground of Webern's mature style. Metaphorically, in a single stride his music has stepped through the looking-glass.

Simply because it *is* a Symphony, this far from perfect work turns up rather too often in concert programmes for its own good, as if, with such a title, it must by definition be the quintessential Webern masterpiece. It is not. The music's slight stiffness of utterance, though an understandable by-product of a first attempt at a new style, is untypical of its composer; and the restrained scoring – for clarinet, bass clarinet, two horns, a harp, and a small string section – does not allow full scope for the multi-faceted transparency that is such a beautiful feature of Webern's later works with orchestra (as also of his earlier ones). But the Symphony is nonetheless the most important single landmark in Webern's lone ascent towards the summit of his composing life.

Down below in his native country, conditions of day-to-day life were becoming steadily more unstable. Mass unemployment, the destructive legacy of Austria's post-war economic and imperial collapse, was about to be exacerbated by the Great Depression that was to decimate the entire industrialized Western world. To make matters even worse the two main political parties, the Social Democrats and the Christian Socials, had each acquired what was in effect a private army roaming the First Austrian Republic. The Heimwehr, which had evolved out of local military resistance to the Yugoslav invasion of Carinthia in 1919, had by now developed into a nationwide anti-Marxist armed front, albeit a loosely interconnected one. In 1923 the socialist wing of the Social Democratic Party had responded by forming the similarly armed Republikanischer Schutzbund (Republican Defence League). Flash points between the two organizations duly proliferated.

Despite these ominous signs of his country's social and economic disintegration, Webern's conducting career continued to prosper. An exception to this otherwise promising scenario was the demise of his association with the Mödlinger Männergesangverein. In May 1926 a soloist engaged for one of their concerts had cancelled due to illness,

Opposite, the Ministry of Justice in Vienna, set on fire during the huge demonstrations against Ignaz Seipel's right-of-centre coalition government on 15–16 July 1927. When the demonstrators would not let fire engines through, police opened fire on the crowd, killing ninety people. The Social Democratic Party organized a general strike in protest; this was suppressed by the government in Vienna and by the Heimwehr in the rest of the country.

and a sizeable section of the chorus had voiced its disapproval at Webern's decision to replace her with a Jewish singer. Webern, unable to accept this refusal to put artistic matters first, resigned after the performance. His successful Workers Symphony Concerts in Vienna were supplemented, however, by a growing number of invitations to appear abroad, where his music, too, had begun to meet with an increasingly positive response. At the International Society for Contemporary Music (ISCM) festival in Zürich in June 1926, the Five Pieces for Orchestra Op. 10 were played for the first time. The general reception was strongly favourable, with one press notice in particular indicating the memorable impression made by this example of Webern's composing at its very best.

Anton Webern raised his baton before a chamber orchestra which included a guitar, mandolin, cowbells, and that horrible instrument, the harmonium. From the silence there escaped into sound wafts of strangely beautiful colour. The ear caught wraith-like wisps of melody which, as smoke, eddied for a moment and then dissolved. A sudden shimmer of iridescence where form and colour became one – and then silence gently withdrew from us that of which we had scarcely become aware. Only a true musical poet could give us these fugitive glimpses of a new and fascinating world of sound.

The extra-curricular hospitality arranged by the festival organizers included an excursion by car along the shores of the Vierwaldstätter-see to the villages of Altdorf and Andermatt. No doubt it had been thoughtfully surmised that this would go down well with an eminent and mountain-loving guest. Unfortunately the Swiss Alps failed to impress Webern, who described them in his diary as 'showcase, not landscape'. The problem evidently was that the mountains, however spectacular, were not Austrian ones.

Important performances were also taking place much further afield. In November 1926 the celebrated conductor Serge Koussevitsky gave the American première of the Five Pieces Op. 10 in New York. The Passacaglia was played by the Philadelphia Orchestra under its charismatic maestro, Leopold Stokowski, in April 1927; in the audience was Ernst Diez, who was lecturing at Bryn Mawr college nearby, and who reported back to his cousin on the occasion. But Webern's music could still also provoke a literally violent response.

A performance of the String Trio by members of the Kolisch String Quartet at the 1928 ISCM festival in Siena was described by Webern in a letter to Schoenberg.

As Kolisch told me, it was like this. During the first measures of the second movement the restlessness became so great that he decided to interrupt. The ensuing demonstrative applause restored quiet, and Kolisch could once again begin the movement and play it to the end. But then things really broke loose, sparked by an Italian critic who declared that he would induce Mussolini *to order the festival broken off. Such music should not be allowed to be played in Italy. Then a German critic, [Hermann] Springer by name, retorted. Immediately after this the Italian critic went at him with his fists. Members of the audience jumped on the podium. At this point [Alfredo] Casella and [Edward] Dent [respectively committee member and president of the ISCM] gave speeches and ordered the* Italian out of the hall. *Whereupon the latter is said to have challenged Casella to a duel …*

Greater satisfaction had earlier come from another landmark occasion involving the Schoenberg circle: in March 1927 Webern conducted the première of Berg's masterly Chamber Concerto for violin, piano, and thirteen wind instruments in the Konzerthaus in Vienna, with Rudolf Kolisch and Eduard Steuermann the two soloists, and with wind players from the Vienna Philharmonic Orchestra. The Webern family's summer holiday that year was spent in a farmhouse at Hafning, a village a few kilometres north of Leoben in the Mur valley in Styria. In an ecstatic entry in Webern's diary, a quotation from Goethe rubs shoulders with scenes of happy domesticity. 'Daily view of the mountains! At all hours, in all types of weather. "… the mysterious clear light, as the highest energy, eternal, singular, and indivisible." … Around six o'clock [in the evening] usually a walk in the Krumpengraben [valley] or in the surrounding forest, looking for mushrooms and berries. Minna and the children take many sunbaths, especially Mali.'

Following page, wayside shrine and crucifix on the Raxalpe, which Webern frequently ascended in 1927–8, with the Schneeberg beyond

Webern's favourite mountain at this time, besides his beloved Hochschwab, was the Schneealpe, one of a group consisting also of the Raxalpe and its neighbouring Schneeberg, ranged like a trio of sentinels guarding the eastern fringes of the Austrian Alps. Lying just

fifty kilometres southwest of Vienna, the three mountains and their exquisite surrounding countryside are perfectly located to assuage the alpine yearnings of semi-impecunious composers and other citizens of Austria's capital. The region is also sacred ground for all card-carrying Schoenbergians: among the foothills to the southeast of the Schneeberg lies the village of Payerbach, where Schoenberg had composed *Verklärte Nacht* while on holiday with Zemlinsky in September 1899. For good measure a cable car ascending to the eastern end of the broad, whaleback ridge of the Raxalpe had been constructed. A delighted Webern took to availing himself regularly of this outrageously convenient means of transport towards the mountain's spacious uplands.

During these years he climbed and reclimbed the Schneealpe and its neighbours, sometimes alone, sometimes in the company of family and friends (Steuermann and the Humpliks among them). Highlights of the summer of 1928 included a journey to Klagenfurt to see his sisters, Maria and Rosa, and to visit the Preglhof and his parents' graves in Schwabegg and Annabichl. There was also a trip to Vordernberg in the mountains to the north of Hafning, to meet up with Ernst Diez on the occasion of his fiftieth birthday; and in August Webern rounded off a highly agreeable summer with yet another ascent of the Hochschwab. Back in Mödling in the early autumn, he embarked busily on new arrangements of two of his earlier works. The first of these, made with logistics of performance in mind, was a re-scoring of the Six Pieces for Orchestra for reduced forces; these, while still large, are not as gargantuan as those of the 1909 original, which are cut back in the new version in favour of a generally enhanced sharpness of orchestral focus. The second arrangement, of the Five Movements for String Quartet in a version for string orchestra, is a more radical alternative to its original model, whose feverish sound-world is developed in the intricate extra detail now made possible by the expanded instrumentation. Webern also began work on a new composition he envisaged as a three-movement concerto for four soloists and string orchestra, an idea modelled on Bach's set of Brandenburg Concertos.

He continued to be kept busy by his teaching and conducting schedule – perhaps too busy, to judge from the onset of a period of illness in October. In early November, exhausted after rehearsing

Schoenberg's unaccompanied chorus *Friede auf Erden* ('Peace on Earth') and Mahler's Second Symphony for a pair of concerts in the Musikvereinsaal, he had to cancel his appearances at the performances. The conductor Erwin Stein, an erstwhile fellow pupil of Schoenberg, stepped capably into the breach, and Webern retreated to Bad Hofgastein in the Salzburg Alps to take a rest cure for the pernicious and unidentifiable stomach illness afflicting him.

Webern rehearsing the Vienna Symphony Orchestra in the Konzerthaus on 23 May 1933 for a performance of Mahler's Sixth Symphony

December found him successfully recuperating at a sanatorium in
Semmering. Back home in Mödling in January 1929, he resumed
both his choral rehearsals and his work on the new 'concerto',
for whose planned third movement – a rondo – he noted down
this outline:

Main themes	Secondary themes	
I		*Coolness of early spring (Anninger, first flora, primroses, anemones, pasque-flowers)*
	I	*Cosy warm sphere of the highest meadows*
II		*Dachstein, snow and ice, crystal-clear air*
	II	*Soldanella, blossoms of the highest region*
III		*The children on ice and snow*
	I	*Repetition of the first secondary theme (sphere of the alpine roses)*
	II	*[Repetition of the] Second secondary theme, light, sky*
IV	*Coda*	*Outlook into the highest region*

(The Anninger is a hill in the Vienna Woods just south of
Mödling; the Dachstein is a spectacular 3,000-metre peak near
Schladming in the Styrian Alps, attempted by Webern first in 1906
and subsequently twice more before he successfully climbed it in July
1930.) The music linked to these impressions went through an
extensive metamorphosis before attaining its final form, some fifteen
months later, as the second movement of a two-movement Quartet
for Violin, Clarinet, Tenor Saxophone, and Piano. It is impossible to
detect here any obvious relationship between the musical ideas
themselves and the vivid memories which evidently caused them to
crystallize. Nonetheless it is clear that as always with Webern,
however 'abstract' his music may seem, there was an absolute
connection between the visual world around him and his private
musical response to it.

His genial mood at this time radiates from a letter to the
Humpliks concerning a portrait bust of himself that had been com-
missioned from the sculptor by the Museum of the City of Vienna.
'Many thanks to friend Humplik for his lovely letter,' wrote Webern.

*Opposite, the Dachstein from
the south; the summit, on the
far left, was climbed by
Webern on 22 July 1930*

KLEINER MUSIKVEREINS-SAAL

Montag, den 13. April 1931
abends halb 8 Uhr

KOLISCH-QUARTETT
EDUARD STEUERMANN

Mitwirkende: Aenne Michalski (Staatsoper). Prof. Johann Löw (Klarinette)
Leopold Wlach (Saxophon)

ANTON WEBERN:

1. Fünf Sätze für Streichquartett, op. 5
   Heftig bewegt - Sehr langsam - Sehr bewegt Sehr langsam In zarter Bewegung

2. Lieder aus op. 3, 4 und 12
   Eingang   Kahl reckt der Baum
   Dies ist ein Lied   Der Tag ist vergangen
   Im Windesweben   Gleich und Gleich

3. Trio für Geige, Bratsche und Violoncello, op. 20
   Sehr langsam — Sehr getragen und ausdrucksvoll; zart bewegt

4. Vier Stücke für Geige und Klavier, op. 7
   Sechs Bagatellen für Streichquartett, op. 9
   Drei kleine Stücke für Violoncello und Klavier, op. 11

5. Quartett für Geige, Klarinette, Tenor-Saxophon und Klavier, op. 22
   Sehr mäßig — Sehr schwungvoll   (Uraufführung)

Klavier: Steinway & Sons, beigestellt von der Firma Bernhard Kohn

Preis: 60 Groschen

Poster announcing the first ever all-Webern concert, including the first performance of the Quartet Op. 22

'I am very glad my skull has at last proved some use to someone. But you'd be ill-advised to let on that it's mine – the deal would be cancelled!' The concerts from which he had been obliged to withdraw the previous November were repeated in April at the Konzerthaus under his direction, with resounding success. Later in 1929 he accepted an invitation to conduct at the BBC in London, which necessitated crossing the English Channel for the first time. ('The sea extremely rough. House-high waves. First felt miserable, but remained firm.') It was during this visit that Webern saw his first talking motion picture – a then far from traditional art-form – by which he was mightily impressed, to judge from a letter written by Eduard Steuermann a few months later to his own sister and brother-in-law (himself a film director).

Today I had a long talk with Webern about films. He is unbelievably enthusiastic about 'talkies' and explained to me how in some film he had seen recently certain moments, gestures, had the same effect on him as 'Neige, Du Schmerzensreiche'. [A reference to Goethe's verse-drama Faust, *Part I.] Even if it is perhaps a momentary over-estimation, I was nevertheless very pleased: such an uninhibited response from someone as highly organized artistically as Webern permits me to believe in a better future humanity … His intense artistic wish would be to write music for a film. Could you perhaps give him an idea? He thinks that … they should have him come to Hollywood …*

Webern had reason to be well disposed to all things American at this time, since the first performance of his Symphony had taken place in December 1929 in New York. Nearer home, as ever, there was Vienna to contend with. Two concerts given on successive evenings within the same building summed up Webern's current stock in his adopted city. On 12 April 1931 he conducted Brahms's *German Requiem* in a Workers Symphony Concert in the Musikvereinsaal, to thunderous acclaim. Next day, having no doubt savoured the glowing press notices, he was among the audience assembled in the small hall of the Musikverein to hear the first-ever concert consisting entirely of his own music, including the première of his new Quartet.

The reviews ranged from dismissive to abusive. 'This work is really a direct offence against good taste,' read one, 'since the squeaking, yelping, and gargling sound-scraps of the clarinet and the saxophone demonstrate amazing similarity to certain vital human utterances of an indecent nature … At least to the listeners with natural sensibilities, this mode of creation signifies a sin against the spirit of tonal art, which up to today, thank God, has remained still sacred to us.' The writer and critic Paul Stefan, a long-standing supporter of the Schoenberg school, professed himself similarly nonplussed, if in more moderate terms.

*These newest formulations, I openly admit, have progressed so far that
I cannot follow them for the time being – they appear to be nothing but
school-like constructions, and only the genius of Webern guarantees that
probably more will have to be sought in them ... This music will
probably never become an art for the masses. But also for the artist, for
the common cause, such isolation can become a danger, a tragedy.*

It seems strange that the mercurial, fantasy-like idiom of the
Quartet – which falls benignly on the ear compared to that of the
more austere Symphony or the formidable String Trio – should have
been found quite so difficult. The problem was perhaps the radical
quality in Webern's twelve-note music which Erwin Stein pinned
down when writing about the new work in the periodical *Anbruch* a
few weeks later: 'The intermediate stages of the development [of each
melodic idea] ... are being omitted; only the essential, the point of
departure and the result, is being said.' Meanwhile, apparently
undismayed by the Quartet's reception, Webern had just completed a
new project – the orchestration, at his publisher's request, of a set of
Six German Dances for piano by Schubert which had recently been
discovered in a Viennese archive. He was characteristically blind to
the project's commercial possibilities and undertook the assignment
for a flat fee rather than on a royalty basis, a decision which
earned him Schoenberg's exasperated rebuke. Sure enough, the
German Dances were to become Webern's most frequently played
'composition' during his lifetime and afterwards.

An idyllic holiday with Wilhelmine in August 1931 included a
four-day hike in the Hohe Tauern through the region around the
Grossglockner, Austria's highest mountain, and a visit to Alban and
Helene Berg at their summer home by the Ossiachersee in Carinthia.
Webern's health nonetheless broke down again in the autumn; the
same mysterious and probably psychosomatic stomach complaint
forced him to cancel another scheduled concert appearance on the
day itself, and he spent most of November undergoing treatment in a
sanatorium near Mödling. Feeling that his constant commuting
between Mödling and Vienna was exacerbating his health problems,
in January 1932 he moved with his family to a second-floor apartment
in the suburb of Hietzing, closer to the city centre. The noise from
the street below, however, unnerved him instantly, and within days he

*Opposite, a modern view
of the church and village
of Heiligenblut, ten kilometres southeast of the
Grossglockner in the Hohe
Tauern, where Webern went
hiking in 1931*

was attempting to move back to the Mödling apartment they had just left, but the landlord, who was about to sell the house, would not agree to a new lease. Too unsettled to compose, Webern instead seized on the opportunity to give a series of private, unscripted lectures on the century's recent musical developments (as seen from the vantage-point of the Schoenberg school) at the home of a Viennese physician and his music-loving wife. Entitled 'The Path to Twelve-Note Composition', the eight weekly lectures were taken down in short-hand at the time by one of the audience, and were later to be included in this form in the posthumously published *The Path to the New Music* (the title of Webern's second series of lectures, given early the following year). It was not until September that Webern was able to escape from Hietzing and move into what was to be his final home: a five-room apartment consisting of the top floor and attic of a two-storey house at Im Auholz 8 in Maria Enzersdorf, immediately next to Mödling. 'At last we will have a garden – and what a sweet one – all to ourselves,' he wrote to the Humpliks in August. '*Directly by a wood!* It is a *cul-de-sac* that leads right up to the mountain slope, ours is the last house. We are happy.'

He had been ill yet again with his nervous stomach ailment, and during his enforced recuperation in the summer had received a bluffly sympathetic letter from Schoenberg.

> I believe ... that it stems from the soul [Gemüt]! I think you get too worked up about everything. Whether it is conducting, holding a rehearsal, having to gain a point, learning of a criticism, or whatever else it may be of countless other things: you always put too much heart into it. (If I did not know this about myself, I should not understand it so well in your case.) I believe: if for half a year you had no annoyance and no agitations ... you would be well. Naturally this is not easy in our profession. Still, it is not quite impossible.

Unable to concentrate on his composing as he liked to every summer, and also prevented from conducting, Webern was nonetheless a model patient and did not attempt to convert his artistic frustration into a state of mind sufficiently fraught to hold up his recovery. After a few weeks of treatment at a sanatorium near Vienna he was sent to the health resort of Bad Fusch in the Hohe Tauern, a few kilometres north of the Grossglockner. As always when in the high mountains, his spirits soared. 'In a tub made of larch wood one lies down in this indescribable [spring] water,' he wrote to Berg. '… I already feel as I did once upon a time in my childhood days. A long-missed feeling.' A fortnight later he was back in Vienna, busy with the move from Hietzing to the apartment in Maria Enzersdorf. With this completed to his satisfaction, he resumed his conducting engagements. One of the most important, at least for posterity, was a visit to Frankfurt in December to conduct the city's Radio Orchestra in a programme including his own arrangement of Schubert's Six German Dances. The result was one of the few recordings that apparently survive of Webern conducting any music composed or arranged by him.

Now, with his professional career at its peak, events on the chessboard of European politics took a fateful turn. The National Socialist party's relentless rise to electoral prominence in Germany in previous years, abetted by its penchant for ruthless street thuggery, had reached a point where in January 1933 its leader, the Austrian-born Adolf Hitler, was asked by Germany's president to form a new cabinet. Hitler dissolved parliament, called new elections, and took advantage of the burning-down of the parliament's Reichstag building to whip up a nationwide crusade against the German left. His party having won a parliamentary majority on 5 March, Hitler immediately set about securing for himself totalitarian powers; and the burgeoning anti-Semitism in every area of German life now became official government policy.

One of the new regime's earliest targets was Schoenberg. He had visited Vienna for what was to be the last time in February 1933, and there had been a happy reunion with his friends and ex-pupils, including Webern. A fortnight later, at a meeting of the senate of the Prussian Academy in Berlin, its president announced that Hitler wished to 'break the Jewish stranglehold' on Western music in general, and on the Academy in particular. Schoenberg, who during the preceding months had been wide awake to the darkening political situation, stormed out of the room with the words: 'You don't need to say this sort of thing to me twice!' He at once made plans to leave Germany as soon as possible.

Propaganda poster, after
regional elections in Tyrol,
announcing the forty-one
per cent vote won by the
Austrian Nazi Party on
23 April 1933. The heading
proclaims 'Hitler's Election
Victory in Austria!'; the
Social Democratic
Party is referred to as the
'Red Death'.

Hitler arriving at a
National Socialist Party
rally at the Lustgarten,
Berlin, 1 May 1934.
Seated beside him in the
car is his Vice Chancellor,
Franz von Papen.

The Reichstag parliament building in Berlin in flames, 27 February 1933. It has never been established whether the fire was a politically convenient accident, or was started deliberately with Hitler's approval to create a pretext for the Nazi Party's attacks on the German left during the general election campaign already under way.

Below, Engelbert Dollfuss, chancellor of Austria from May 1932 until his assassination in July 1934, photographed during a state visit to Rome in 1933. Dollfuss stands at the centre of the group's front row; to the right (on Dollfuss's left) is Benito Mussolini, *Duce* of Italy.

Webern responded to these happenings with genuine outrage, making his feelings quite clear in an impromptu preface to the fourth of his new series of weekly lectures, *The Path to the New Music*, on 14 March.

> *What's going on in Germany at the moment amounts to the destruction of spiritual life! Let's look at our own [musical] territory! It's interesting that the alterations as a result of the Nazis affect almost exclusively musicians, and one can imagine what's still to come ... What will happen next? To Schoenberg, for instance? And though at present it's linked with anti-Semitism, later on it will be impossible to appoint anyone capable even if he isn't a Jew! Nowadays 'cultural Bolshevism' is the name given to everything that's going on around Schoenberg, Berg, and myself ... Imagine what will be destroyed, wiped out, by this hate of culture!*
>
> *...It's so difficult to shake off politics, because they're a matter of life and death. – But that makes it all the more urgent a duty to save what can be saved ... Now we are not far off a state when you land in prison* simply because you're a serious artist! *Or rather, it's happened already! – I don't*

Schoenberg in the early
1930s

*know what Hitler understands by 'new music', but I know that for those
people what we mean by it is a crime. The moment is not far off when
one will be locked up for writing such things. At the very least one's
thrown to the wolves, made an economic sacrifice.*

*Will they still come to their senses at the eleventh hour? If not,
spiritual life faces an abyss.*

Webern suggested to Schoenberg that he might come and live
again in Mödling. Schoenberg, however, refused to entertain the
slightest doubt as to Hitler's long-term intentions regarding Austria's
absorption into a Greater Germany, and with it the near-certain
consequences for himself and his family. Having formally re-
embraced Judaism at a ceremony in Paris in July, he spent the rest of
the summer in France and then, in October, crossed the Atlantic to
New York with his wife and seventeen-month-old daughter. In
1934 they settled in California where Schoenberg, at first making a
living by teaching private pupils, was appointed professor at the
University of California at Los Angeles in 1936. He was never to
return to Europe.

The effect in Austria of Hitler's rise to power was to trigger a
sequence of events that were to bring the country's simmering political cauldron to boiling-point. Since May 1932 the Austrian
chancellor had been Engelbert Dollfuss, who headed an uneasy
parliamentary coalition with a tiny overall majority, in which his own
Christian Socials were the largest party. Besides the Social Democrats
on the left, Dollfuss had to cope with the increasing electoral
strength of the Austrian National Socialists, whose brand of storm-
trooping Nazism was so violent that even Hitler was to find them
virtually uncontrollable. Determined to preserve Austria's
independence, Dollfuss relied increasingly for his power-base on the
armed Heimwehr at home, and on Mussolini's dubious and
manipulative support from abroad. (The Italian dictator was finding
Austria a useful component in his expansionist power-plays regarding
France and Germany.) Taking advantage of a technical impasse in
the voting procedure of the Austrian parliament in March 1933,
Dollfuss suspended the democratic process and assumed dictatorial
powers. An immediate consequence was his outlawing of the Social
Democrats' armed Republikanischer Schutzbund.

Now, with the National Socialists in power in Germany, the pressure on the Dollfuss regime mounted relentlessly. Nazi-instigated terrorism became increasingly widespread, while the pan-German appeal of the Austrian National Socialist Party gathered further popular support; in local elections in Tyrol in April, for instance, it won forty-one per cent of the vote. In June, Dollfuss declared the party illegal. This did not prevent an increasing number of Webern's compatriots from continuing to join it, including his own son Peter, who was to do so apparently without his father's knowledge while working in the firm of his future brother-in-law in Graz. Both Mussolini and the Heimwehr, meanwhile, were pressing for the elimination of the Social Democrats altogether as a political force.

Still Webern's creative and professional lives held to their course with barely ruffled serenity. He began composing a group of songs for

Webern and friends at a mountain hut on the Schneealpe, June 1933: (from left) Ernst Diez, Webern, Josef Hueber, Josef Polnauer

Engelbert Dollfuss (1892–1934) at a rally in Vienna of the Fascist-style Fatherland Front, formed by him in 1933. The symbol on the banners is the *Kruckenkreuz* ('Crutched Cross'), the Front's equivalent of the German Nazi Party's swastika.

The rising of the Austrian Social Democratic Party's armed Republikanischer Schutzbund, 12–16 February 1934. *Above*, street sign in Vienna warning, 'Keep back or you will be shot'.
Left, Government troops cordon off a street in Vienna.

voice and piano to texts by Hildegard Jone, while continuing work on a project that had started out early in 1931 as an orchestral piece, and was now finding its final shape as a Concerto for piano and chamber group. The summer's delights included a trip to the Schneealpe in June with a quartet of close colleagues: Ernst Diez; the singer Josef Hueber; Webern's pupil Ludwig Zenk; and Josef Polnauer, one of Schoenberg's and Webern's oldest friends from pre-war days, who had been a loyal and enthusiastic mainstay of the Society for Private Musical Performances. Webern's fiftieth birthday in December was marked by a number of performances of his music at home and abroad, and by a special issue of the Viennese periodical *23* consisting of tributes from his friends and supporters, and of articles on his music.

In January he began rehearsing Bach's St John Passion with the Singverein chorus for a concert in Vienna. Then, on 12 February 1934, the leader of the Linz branch of the now illegal Republikanischer Schutzbund resisted demands to allow a police search for arms. When reinforcements arrived, the Schutzbund members opened fire. The fighting spread to Vienna, Graz, Steyr and other towns; Dollfuss ordered the army to use artillery against centres of resistance in a housing estate in Vienna. When the uprising had been suppressed four days later, 196 people had been killed on the Social Democrats' side and 118 on the government's.

Dollfuss immediately outlawed the Social Democratic Party, reorganized those areas of Viennese local government which it had hitherto continued to run, and abolished most of its institutions, including the Kunststelle, which was responsible for both the Workers Symphony Concerts and those given by the Singverein chorus. At a stroke, Webern had lost his two largest sources of income and the twin pillars of his professional success for over a decade.

6

Webern in 1935. The scarf, a Christmas present from his daughter Amalie, was one of his treasured possessions.

I would like to attempt to tell you what moves me increasingly and always more urgently in these days when it becomes ever darker and darker: the sense of accountability! Will the question not be posed: 'And where were you in these times?' I have the feeling that it becomes more and more decisive!

Webern to Schoenberg, July 1934

The Sunlight Speaks 1934–45

It took Webern a few days to realize the scale of the disaster that had overtaken his conducting career. As the seriousness of the situation began to sink in, his bewilderment led him as usual to think of looking to Schoenberg for support, and the fact that Schoenberg was now in America seems to have been behind Webern's sudden interest – for all his devotion to his beloved Austrian *Heimat* – in the idea of emigrating to the new world on the far side of the Atlantic Ocean. Schoenberg, for all his difficulties in earning a living during his first American winter by teaching in Boston and New York, had painted a picture in his letters of a musical climate altogether more receptive toward his, Berg's and Webern's brand of composition than had ever existed in Vienna; referring to a forthcoming engagement to conduct his own string-orchestra arrangement of *Verklärte Nacht* in Chicago, he remarked dryly to Webern that 'hereabouts this is a sort of Tchaikovsky piece'. A few weeks after the suppression of the Social Democrat uprising Webern wrote to Adolph Weiss, the American composer and former Schoenberg pupil who had helped to arrange the première of Webern's Symphony in New York five years earlier.

From Schoenberg came, thank God, highly enjoyable news, but the activity over there is probably very strenuous for him. Otherwise I am happy over it and wish very much for myself also to be able to be in America soon*.!!! … For here it becomes more and more difficult for me. As a result of the events at which I hinted, I have lost my chorus and with it a fine sphere of activity that I have toiled to build up and enlarge for a* decade *… There is virtually no prospect that the organization will be restored as it last existed. What they have destroyed for me, dear friend! With cannons! We were just studying the* St John Passion*!*

To make matters worse, a number of planned conducting engagements abroad also came to nothing. All that Webern now had to live on were fees from a few private pupils and the minuscule royalties earned by performances of his music. Even the conducting work offered him in recent years by Austrian Radio dried up almost entirely, since his long-standing association with Social Democrat cultural institutions now made him politically unacceptable to the broadcasting hierarchy. (The irony was that the association had never been official; Webern, who had always disliked explicit party-political standpoints, had in 1929 turned down the offer of a senior post in the music department of Austrian Radio mainly because this would have involved a direct connection with the Social Democratic Party.) On top of all these problems, Webern's daughter Amalie had recently undergone a costly operation to deal with a kidney ailment that had plagued her for years. An American friend and former pupil, Mark Brunswick, at this time heard of his ex-teacher's financial difficulties. Over the next few months Brunswick's regular donations, supplemented by Webern's occasional guest-conducting (including another concert at the BBC in London), meant that the household in Maria Enzersdorf was just able to make ends meet. Webern himself, meanwhile, decided to make the most of his unscheduled surplus of time by settling down to composition.

He had produced only two works in the past six years, the Symphony in 1928 and the Quartet in 1930; he now completed another three within just nine months. This surge of sustained creativity seems to have banished from his mind further thoughts of emigration, which in any case would have amounted to an exercise in psychological and creative upheaval of which he would probably have proved incapable. In that sense, the music that Webern wrote in the spring and summer of 1934 amounts to a spiritual homecoming of the truest and deepest kind. From now until the end of his *Heimat*-rooted life he was to compose slowly, but steadily and surely, a sequence of masterworks which inhabit a world increasingly remote from the terrestrial disasters that were to unfold around him. As Hildegard Jone had perceptively written a few months beforehand in a tribute to mark her friend's fiftieth birthday: 'What is expressed in Anton Webern's music is no longer description; it is the penetrating radiant force of the heart.'

By then Webern had already composed his first settings of Jone's poetry; these were to become the second and third of his Three Songs from *Viae inviae* of Hildegard Jone, Op. 23, for voice and piano.

In March 1934 he completed this set and began a second cycle of Jone settings, also for voice and piano, which he finished in November and designated as Three Songs Op. 25. In September he had also completed – just in time to dedicate the work to Schoenberg on his sixtieth birthday – the Concerto for Piano and Chamber Group which had begun life as a projected orchestral piece three years earlier. All three works sound if anything even more idiosyncratic and un-Schoenbergian than their immediate predecessors. They also demonstrate Webern's increasingly assured and singular mastery of the twelve-note method in quite distinct ways.

The two sets of songs represent Webern's return, for the first time in twenty years, to the voice-and-piano medium which had inspired some of his finest work as a young composer. Their spare, uncluttered lyricism fuses twelve-note technique with an unambiguously traditional approach to vocal writing: a combination which is beautiful in its own right, and which also inhabits a quite different stylistic planet from the transcendent experimentalism of many of Webern's middle-period songs. The three-movement Concerto, on the contrary, is a trenchantly radical piece whose tautness of argument and inner construction extends to the nature of the work's twelve-note row itself. This actually consists of a three-note row followed by its retrograde inversion, retrograde, and inversion, with each of these note-cells transposed (i.e., placed at higher or lower pitch-levels) so that they also fit within a single twelve-note unit: a musical image of unity-within-unity of a kind that had come to fascinate Webern. (A prototype of the idea had already occurred in the Symphony, where the second six notes of the twelve-note row are a transposed retrograde of the first six.)

Unlike much advanced twentieth-century music, the Concerto is written in a way which makes this preoccupation with its note-row's atom-structure immediately audible. The myriad three-note constellations spin freely around each other in the quick first movement. In the slow second one they then assemble into a single melodic line over the piano's accompaniment, with the component notes or note-groups of the melody parcelled out among different instruments (a device first explored by Webern in his Six Pieces for Orchestra Op. 6, and here as there conveying not so much an effect of fragmentation as a sense of the lyrical impulse that sparks across the gaps between the notes). The quick third movement, again compressing the three-note groups into impacted units, charges along with Beethovenian impetuousness. Altogether the Concerto amounts to the most striking musical sound-object that Webern had yet composed.

His summer of peaceful creativity was not mirrored in the continuing downward spiral of the political situation around him. In July the Austrian National Socialists attempted, almost certainly without Hitler's knowledge, an armed putsch aimed at seizing the entire Austrian government in Vienna. It was foiled, though not before Dollfuss had been assassinated by the conspirators. Despite simultaneous risings by local Nazi organizations throughout the country, the army and the Heimwehr quickly regained control of the situation, and the education minister, Kurt Schuschnigg, took over as chancellor; but the incident had further underlined the First Republic's near-terminal instability. Hitler, mindful of Mussolini's continuing support (temporarily) for Austrian independence and of similarly voiced concern by France and Britain, announced that he had no intention of interfering in Austria's internal affairs, still less of annexing the country to Germany.

Kurt Schuschnigg, Austrian chancellor from July 1934 to March 1938 (left), with Mussolini (centre) at the Palazzo Venezia in Rome, November 1934; on the right is Egon Berger-Waldenegg, the Austrian foreign minister.

Webern meanwhile remained unflinchingly loyal to his colleagues with Social Democrat connections, notably David Josef Bach, who after the previous February's events had been dismissed from his post as organizer of the Workers Symphony Concerts. On the way back from an unsuccessful attempt with Ludwig Zenk and Josef Hueber to climb the Wildspitze, the highest peak of the Ötztal Alps in Tyrol, Webern called on Bach where he was staying by the Wallersee near Salzburg, and in honour of Bach's sixtieth birthday presented him with a copy of his own Two Songs on texts by Goethe, along with a collection of messages of goodwill and support. Back in Vienna, he began work on a welcome commission from his publishers. By January 1935 he had completed an arrangement for small orchestra of the six-part Ricercar – a strict and complex form of counterpoint – from Johann Sebastian Bach's collection of instrumental pieces entitled *A Musical Offering*. Webern's sonically remarkable re-thinking of this intricate and cerebral work is an explicit homage to a composer he revered. It also develops his own Concerto's mosaic-like approach to instrumentation with an even more insistent radicalism.

In February, casting around in Hildegard Jone's writings for something suitable for a choral work, he alighted on the poem *Das Augenlicht* ('The Light of the Eye') from her *Viae inviae* cycle, and by September had completed a setting of this for chorus and chamber orchestra. He dedicated the new work to his daughter Amalie as a wedding present; the previous month she had married Gunter Waller, a young businessman whose parents lived at Im Auholz 2, just down the road from the Weberns. (Amalie later recalled how her mother and father, tremendously proud of their daughter and determined not to give the well-off Waller family any excuse to look down on them, laid on a much more elaborate wedding reception than they could realistically afford.) Meeting up at the wedding with his sister Maria Clementschitsch and her husband Paul, Webern needed little persuasion to join his brother-in-law in an attempt six days later to climb one of Austria's mightiest peaks, the 3,674-metre Grossvenediger in the Hohe Tauern. Much to Webern's delight, the ascent was successful.

On his way back to Vienna he visited Alban Berg who, composing at feverish speed in his *Waldhaus* (forest house) retreat by the Ossiachersee, had just completed a commission from the American

Opposite, looking southwest towards the outlying mountains of the Grossvenediger range in the Hohe Tauern: the Grossvenediger itself is a further ten kilometres beyond.

violinist Louis Krasner. This was a Violin Concerto dedicated
'To the memory of an angel', the 'angel' being Manon Gropius, the
enchantingly beautiful daughter of Alma Mahler (widow of Gustav,
and the dedicatee of *Wozzeck*) by her second marriage to the architect
Walter Gropius. The eighteen-year-old Manon had died in April
from infantile paralysis; and Berg himself was unwell at this time,
having completed the concerto while suffering from an abscess –
caused by an insect sting at the base of his spine – which was
refusing to heal.

Back at Maria Enzersdorf, and resuming his impecunious working
existence with a purposeful serenity that belied his bleak financial
outlook, Webern was soon busy with a new piece for solo piano. He
had no sources of even vaguely regular income apart from payments
from pupils and his position as a kind of official 'listener-in' to music
programmes on Austrian Radio. In a broadcast concert for that
institution in July he had chosen to conduct Mendelssohn's Violin
Concerto and his own arrangement of the Bach Ricercar (of which he
had already given the world première at the BBC in London in April).
Since the nineteenth-century German composer Mendelssohn had
been Jewish, and the music of the Schoenberg camp had already
been denounced by Joseph Goebbels's Ministry of Propaganda in
Germany as 'degenerate', Webern could not possibly have undertaken
a more tactically disastrous exercise in programme-planning. He was
never to conduct for Austrian Radio again.

The ISCM festival that year was held in September in Prague,
whose cultural life was still outside Dr Goebbels's remit. Among the
audience at the first performance of Webern's new Concerto,
conducted by Heinrich Jalowetz, was the gifted thirty-year-old Italian
composer Luigi Dallapiccola. Deeply impressed, Dallapiccola wrote
in his diary: 'Every decorative element [in the music] has been
eliminated … I could not form a precise idea of the work, it is too
difficult for me to understand; however it seems to represent, without
question, an entire world.' As president of the ISCM's Austrian section
Webern had already undertaken to visit Barcelona over the new year,
to assist with planning the 1936 festival to be held there. Then, on 17
December, Alban Berg was admitted to a Viennese hospital for an
operation to try to counter the infection that had afflicted him since

Josef Goebbels, Hitler's
Minister of Propaganda, at
a National Socialist Party
rally in Berlin in 1933,
right, and, *below*, after
polling during the German
plebiscite of 19 August
1934, in which an eighty-
eight per cent majority
voted for the offices of
president and chancellor to
be combined in that of
Führer of the National
Socialist Party

Covers of exhibition catalogues concerning Nazi-designated 'Degenerate Music', (that of Schoenberg and his circle included), *above,* and 'Degenerate Art', *right.* The lapel badge caricatures the 'Star of David' compulsorily worn by Jews in the Third Reich; the word *Kunst* (Art) is in ironic inverted commas.

the summer. His condition suddenly and rapidly worsened, and he died of general septicaemia on 24 December at the age of fifty.

Like most others who had been to visit Berg in hospital, Webern had not fully understood the seriousness of his friend's illness. Utterly devastated, he nonetheless left for Barcelona on 26 December as planned, missing the funeral at Hietzing cemetery two days later, but all the more determined to ensure that the ISCM would include the première of the new Violin Concerto in the 1936 festival. This achieved, he agreed to conduct the performance himself. On his return to Vienna, an equally saddened Schoenberg wrote to him from California:

> *It is too horrible. There goes one of us (who were only a mere three), and now we two must bear this isolation alone. And the saddest aspect is – it had to be the one of us who had success, who at least could have enjoyed that …*

Alban Berg, c. 1930

In the months before the planned première of Berg's concerto on 19 April, Krasner and a traumatized Webern worked exhaustively on its preparation. Then, as the prospect of the journey to Barcelona loomed, Webern began to show ominous signs of reverting to his conducting-related neurosis of earlier years. When he suddenly announced that he would not go through with the performance, Krasner was only able to make him change his mind by insisting that he himself would not play the solo part either unless Webern was on the podium. The two then made the long train journey together to Spain, where there ensued the most spectacular débâcle of Webern's conducting career. In the face of language difficulties with the Catalan orchestra, his professional rationality went to pieces. So obsessive was his insistence on the minutest rehearsal of every phrase of Berg's concerto that by the end of two of the three scheduled rehearsal periods, only the first four pages of the 76-page score had been covered.

At the start of the third session Krasner and the orchestra pleaded with Webern at least to give them a chance of playing through the whole work. Despite agreeing to do so, Webern still proceeded at the same meticulous snail's pace for a further half hour. Then he suddenly snatched the score from the conducting stand, rushed from the hall, fled to his hotel room, and locked himself in. The crisis culminated in the spectacle of Berg's widow, who had managed to persuade Webern to let her in, literally kneeling at his feet and begging him at least to give up the score so that someone else could conduct the concerto. Eventually and very reluctantly Webern agreed, and the German conductor Hermann Scherchen, having worked on the music with Krasner overnight, took over the première after just one additional rehearsal. Reports of the concert are unanimous as to the memorable impact made by Berg's requiem-like work. Krasner believed that the intensity of the occasion owed much to Webern's impossibly over-dedicated rehearsing, the idealistic spirit of which nonetheless carried over to the performance itself.

Webern had planned to travel with Krasner directly from Barcelona to London, where he was due to conduct the concerto's British première at the BBC on 1 May. Instead, feeling a near-pathological need to reorientate himself amongst the familiar sur-roundings of his Austrian *Heimat*, he journeyed straight home to the

house in Maria Enzersdorf and to a no doubt rather startled
Wilhelmine. He then set off for London as planned, where he
rehearsed the BBC Symphony Orchestra – who were admittedly more
familiar with Webern's ways than their Catalan counterparts had been
– with exemplary self-control. The performance that resulted was a
marvel of incandescent music-making, as is evident from the off-the-
air recording that was made at Krasner's instigation.

The impression given by this bizarre sequence of events – that
Webern as a practical musician amounted to a rare species of
pedagogic lunatic – is contradicted by another artist who worked
with him closely at this time. Having completed his Piano Variations
in September 1936, Webern dedicated the new work to Eduard
Steuermann, who for years had almost as a matter of course been the
first performer of the Schoenberg circle's new works involving piano.
He had also been one of Webern's closest personal friends.
Steuermann, however, was as alert to the forthcoming likely fate of
Jews living in Austria as Schoenberg had been. By the time the
Variations were completed he too, like thousands of others, had left
for America.

The première was therefore given by Peter Stadlen, a young
Austrian pianist who had recently distinguished himself in Webern's
eyes by his coolness under fire when performing in Schoenberg's Suite
for Piano and Chamber Group at the 1937 Venice Biennale festival.
(As the players prepared themselves for the third of the work's four
movements, the hitherto persistent undercurrent of vocal protest
from the Italian audience now surged so ominously that Stadlen's
cellist colleague leaned across to him and enquired: 'Meinen Sie
wirklich?' [Do you really think we should?] Stadlen nonetheless led
the performance firmly to its conclusion.) In the weeks leading up to
the Variations' première Webern several times journeyed into Vienna
to coach the young pianist with his usual assiduous thoroughness.
Stadlen remembers Webern as a charming man, meticulously
concerned that the expressive detail lying behind the music's spare
surface notation should be brought out to maximum effect. (Stadlen
never met Wilhelmine, who in her self-effacing way preferred to keep
clear of this side of her husband's professional life and would stay at
home in Maria Enzersdorf.) The first performance of the Variations
on 27 October 1937 was the last occasion that any of Webern's music

was publicly played in Vienna during his lifetime. By then he had begun to compose a String Quartet, whose intersection of concentrated expression with maximum structural control – as in the similarly approachable Piano Variations – is a hallmark of all his later music.

At this time Webern, like millions of his compatriots, was unaware of the extent to which the fate of the First Austrian Republic had been sealed by the nightmarish European power-games developing around it. Italy's invasion of Abyssinia (now Ethiopia) in October 1935 – the latest of Mussolini's grandiose and impetuous nationalistic escapades – had met with outright condemnation by most of the other Western powers in the League of Nations. Schuschnigg's Austrian government, however, felt compelled to support the only major ally it had, so that Austria now became even more isolated internationally than before. The outcry over Abyssinia led Mussolini to decide that closer relations between Italian Fascism and Hitler's resurgent Germany would be an expedient course of action. The establishment of the Rome–Berlin Axis in October 1936 duly removed from Austria even the mixed blessing of Italian support. From now on there was little to stand in the way of relentless National Socialist pressure on the Austrian state.

The conflicting national emotions that had for so long surged within the hearts of generations of home-loving, peaceably-minded, German-speaking Austrians – *Heimat*-related patriotism on one hand, and a broader sense of pan-German identity on the other – had come to provide an ideal breeding-ground for every shade of political partisanship; after all, if the one set of values could not be invoked successfully, the other always could. Much of the hideously effective appeal of National Socialism in Austria, as in Germany, was rooted in its skill in addressing the post-war grievances of the German-speaking world on several levels at once. Working-class resentment at mass unemployment, largely precipitated by the Allied powers' punitive peace terms after the First World War; middle-class fear at the rise of left-wing influence, relating directly to these desperate social conditions; the subtle and corrosive yearning for some sort of trans-muted return to the imperial glories of the past – the gospel according to Adolf Hitler seemed to offer a potent kind of hope on all these fronts. And the fact that anti-Semitism transcended political and social barriers at every level of German and Austrian society made it the ideal lubricant for the machinery of mass national psychosis, which once again now began to whirr into operation with horrifying speed and comprehensiveness. Millions of Germans and Austrians, however divided among themselves in respect of background, political beliefs, or income-level, could at least agree that it had all been the fault of the Jews.

In the early stages of the First World War, Webern – like almost everyone around him – had been swept up in the prevailing mood of pan-German militarism. In his case this had since given way to an instinctive, though non-ideological sympathy with the artistic policies of the Austrian Social Democrats (themselves an incipiently pan-German party, though from a revolutionary rather than a Fascist standpoint). Now, with the rise of the Third Reich, Webern began to revert once again to his absorption in the idea of a Greater Germany. By mid-1936 he had convinced himself that the First Austrian Republic could only benefit from National Socialism's record in restoring 'order' to the chronically unstable post-war German state; that this would not, and did not, presuppose organized anti-Semitism; and that Nazism's jackbooted methods would in any case be mellowed by the responsibilities of political power. (Richard Strauss, who had a Jewish daughter-in-law, had earlier tried to cling to the same view that the strutting ruthlessness of Germany's new political masters would soon 'blow over'. Like other Aryan Germans with Jewish relatives he was promptly disillusioned in that respect.) Webern is even reported as having asserted that the advent of Nazi control would at last ensure a suitable level of official recognition for Mahler's music in Austria: a quite staggering feat of self-delusion, given that Mahler himself had been Jewish. It was not long before several of Webern's oldest and closest friends, notably David Josef Bach and Eduard Steuermann, had become angered by his view-point. Others, such as Josef Polnauer and the geographically distant Schoenberg, found themselves better able to tolerate Webern's capacity for disingenuous simple-mindedness when it came to contemporary politics.

Early in 1938 the annexation of Austria suddenly moved to the top of Hitler's priorities. The Austrian National Socialists' campaign of violent destabilization had reached a point where the Schuschnigg

Opposite, the Anschluss *(Annexation) of Austria: German troops march through Innsbruck, Tyrol, 12 March 1938*

government was widely seen to be no longer in control of the
country. Schuschnigg himself, at last realizing the pointlessness of
playing for time regarding Germany's intentions, announced on
9 March that a plebiscite on Austria's independence was to be held
four days later. The German dictator saw his opportunity; on the
pretext that the plebiscite was a provocation, he instructed the
German army to prepare to invade Austria, and asked the ever unpre-
dictable Mussolini for his agreement not to intervene. Hermann
Goering, Hitler's Reichsmarschall and principal lieutenant, tele-
phoned the Austrian head of state, President Miklas, to insist on
Schuschnigg's resignation. Schuschnigg, apparently without Miklas's
approval, agreed to step down. Even the threat of *Anschluss*
(annexation), however, did not persuade Miklas to appoint a prominent pro-Nazi cabinet member as chancellor in his place. Having
received Mussolini's assent, Hitler ordered the German army across
the Austrian border on 12 March. Tens of thousands of cheering
Austrians lined Hitler's triumphal route – via his birthplace in
Braunau – to Vienna, where on 14 March huge crowds greeted his
entry into the city. The church bells rang.

On 11 March Webern had listened with Louis Krasner to the
broadcast of Schuschnigg's farewell address to the nation. Next day, as
the German troops goose-stepped their way across his country, he
wrote to the Humpliks: 'I am totally immersed in my work and
cannot, cannot be disturbed.' A marginal note among the sketches for
his String Quartet reads simply: '13 March, incorporation of Austria
into the German Reich.' (A year later even the name of his country
would disappear, and Austria would become the province of
Ostmark.) Along with all other officially designated manifestations of
'degenerate' art, public performance of Webern's music was banned.
Neither this nor the brutality immediately shown by the new regime
towards Austria's Jewish population – who were 'encouraged' to
emigrate as long as they left behind all their property, possessions and
money – made any apparent difference to Webern's outward
acceptance of the *Anschluss*. Heinrich Jalowetz was one of his Jewish
friends who escaped at this time, making his way to America.
Webern's daughter Maria had for years been in love with a Jewish
man; he too now fled abroad.

On the other hand Webern also did nothing to ingratiate himself with the post-*Anschluss* regime, as many others with previous Social Democrat connections were to in the years to come. Had he too done so, he would most likely have been able at least to resurrect his conducting career. But no. Now – as many years ago he had asserted in a different context – one must live only for Art.

He was proud and delighted when the news reached him of the highly successful première on 17 June of his choral work *Das Augenlicht*, in the opening concert of the 1938 ISCM festival at the Queen's Hall in London. (Since the society's Austrian section had been suspended after the *Anschluss*, Webern was unable to attend officially, and as a composer of 'degenerate music' he would probably

Hitler's arrival in Austria was enthusiastically welcomed by many; Webern's daughter Christine and her fiancé were both among the young admirers of the Nazi party.

have been prevented from travelling abroad in any case by the new regime.) A salient part of the success was due to Hermann Scherchen, who by all accounts conducted a wonderful performance. Again in the audience was Luigi Dallapiccola, who penned an assessment of the new work in his diary entry later the same evening:

> *The orchestral forces are limited to essentials … Sonority, colour, articulation, instrumental layout – all is* invention*: every bit as important, therefore, as overall construction.*
>
> Das Augenlicht, *when one hears it, proves full of harmonious poetry: voices and instruments, often with enormous empty spaces between them, create opposing planes of sound. The score seems enriched by those mysterious vibrations which would arise if it were performed under a glass bell-jar … Certain subtleties in the writing would deserve a discussion in themselves: the way, for instance, that Webern avoids as far as possible that brusque 'recall to reality' represented by the strong beat of a bar, which here would break the dream-like atmosphere that permeates the highly poetic composition.*

Webern's music had not yet attained universal acceptance, however, on the far side of the English Channel. The strongly positive press reviews of *Das Augenlicht*'s première pleased him rather more than news of an incident that had taken place also in London six weeks earlier, during a performance of his String Trio at the Wigmore Hall. A few seconds into the opening movement the cellist stopped, said 'Oh, I can't play this thing', and walked off the platform, to be followed shortly by his two abandoned colleagues.

Another less than ideally harmonious event, this time concerning Webern's family, took place in June 1938. His daughter Christine – nineteen years old, five months pregnant, and a member of the Bund deutscher Mädchen, the female counterpart of the Hitler Youth – married Benno Mattel, who wore his brown-shirted Nazi Party uniform for the occasion. The rest of the family had apparently disliked Benno from the start. It was Eduard Steuermann who, in a letter to Webern's biographer Hans Moldenhauer written in 1964, gave the simplest and possibly the most accurate assessment of the cast of mind behind his former friend's apparent complicity with the precepts of the Third Reich.

Unfortunately, the ties of our friendship became rather loose since Hitler's invasion of Austria, as Webern did not react in the way I had a right to expect. Maybe it was unavoidable as so many members of his family were Nazis (some ones more, some ones less), but it made it impossible for me not to change my feelings, at a time when so many of my friends, my pupils and members of my family were murdered.

Several of Webern's friends, too, had become convinced National Socialists, among them Ludwig Zenk. With hindsight it is easy to accuse Webern of craven connivance in the post-*Anschluss* order. It is also probable that most of those same accusers, if finding themselves actually living in a society bristling with Nazi sympathizers and informers, would have been among the first to decide to keep their heads down as Webern did.

In July 1938, encouraged by the success of *Das Augenlicht*, he began composing what was to become the central movement of a more ambitious vocal work, his First Cantata for soprano, chorus, and orchestra. 'A sort of symphony with vocal sections' was how he described the Cantata to Hildegard Jone when it was still in its early stages. It is perhaps Webern's most beautiful creation in its synthesis of his most deeply held artistic values: Renaissance-like purity and unity of construction, Bachian purity of musical thought, the vivid beauty of the natural world, and a consuming love of word-setting. Robert Craft, the American conductor who presided over the first complete recording of Webern's works with opus numbers, has perceptively pointed out that the soprano's culminating solo in the Cantata's third and last movement – a setting of Hildegard Jone's hymn to charity as the highest of the three graces – is an unmistakably operatic moment, and one that echoes back through the years to the young Webern's burning, Maeterlinck-inspired desire to compose for the stage. Webern himself summed up the character of this wondrous movement in a letter written to the Humpliks after its completion. 'Musically, there is not a single centre of gravity in this piece. The harmonic construction … is such that everything is floating.'

Apart from his private teaching and his listening-in work for Austrian Radio, the composition of the Cantata occupied him for the rest of 1938 and for most of the following year. Money was too tight

for any but the briefest of summer holidays in 1939, into which
Webern fitted a visit to Ernst Diez in Vordernberg. When his
daughter Maria asked to go to England to see her Jewish friend before
he emigrated to Australia, Webern arranged for an advance on the
forthcoming publication of his String Quartet (by the London firm of
Boosey and Hawkes) to be paid to her when she arrived, and also
asked David Josef Bach – who had settled in London in January – to
look after her while she was there. Maria returned home in mid-
August. Three weeks later Germany invaded Poland and ignored an
ultimatum from Britain and France to withdraw. On 3 September,
Europe was once again at war.

Manuscript of the opening
bars of the second move-
ment of Webern's First
Cantata, Op. 29.
The text, *Kleiner Flügel
Ahornsamen* ('Little
winged seed of maple'),
is by Hildegard Jone.

By the time that the First Cantata was completed in November 1939, Webern's listening-in position with Austrian Radio had been terminated. Universal Edition, his Viennese publishers, from now on provided him with just enough intermittent work – proof-reading, making piano reductions of other composers' scores, and assessing submitted compositions – to keep going. His children Maria and Peter, both employed in their brother-in-law Gunter Waller's business but living at home, helped out with their pay-packets, and Wilhelmine's mother also contributed small but regular sums. But apart from visits to Winterthur and Basel in neutral Switzerland to hear some concerts featuring his music, Webern's artistic isolation was now virtually complete.

Exactly as at the start of the First World War twenty-five years earlier, the whirlwind early successes of the German army now inspired him to a mood of unrestrained pan-German chauvinism. Josef Hueber, who had been called up and posted to France after the German army's spectacularly rapid conquest of that country in June 1940, had presented Webern with a copy of Hitler's autobiography *Mein Kampf* ('My Struggle'). The contents of this, along with those of the German newsreels, engendered a sequence of letters to Hueber which make appalling reading, written as they were by one of the most intelligent and cultured Austrian artists of the twentieth century.

'The book has brought me much enlightenment,' he wrote in March 1940. '… I see it coming, the pacification of the entire world. At first east of the Rhine as far as – yes, how far? This will depend on the USA. But probably as far as the Pacific Ocean!' In May, after Germany had overrun Norway and Denmark, Hueber was sent another lengthy screed. In part this would seem to have been motivated by Webern's familiar tendency to try to impress by over-emphatically agreeing with a friend's views. The letter is nonetheless unambiguous regarding his views on the accomplishments of the Führer of the Third Reich.

And are things not going forwards with giant steps?! (These last results! Magnificent!) But not only the outward process! Also the inner one! It is elevating! … Since … the Weekly News, *too, is now shown in a new, quite excellent manner, I left the cinema with the definite feeling: yes, if*

the audience is not totally insensitive, then such an evening would really
have to have a purifying effect on the people ... This is Germany today!
But the National Socialist *one, to be sure! Not just any one! This is*
exactly the new *state, for which the seed was already laid twenty years*
ago. Yes, a new state it is, *one that has never existed before!!* It is
something new! *Created by this unique man!!!*

Webern also turned again to the writings of Stefan George, and
delightedly found a parallel between the poet's self-styled brand of
theosophy – prophesying the coming of a future leader who would
create a new imperial order out of chaos – and the subsequent rise
of Hitler.

None of this, meanwhile, prevented him from inviting Josef
Polnauer to dinner at Im Auholz 8 every Friday evening, despite the
fact that social contact between Jews and Aryans had been expressly
forbidden. If these meetings had come to official Party notice,
Webern would quite probably have been sent to a concentration
camp; any number of others were sent for less. Polnauer kept up his
side of the friendship until he eventually went into hiding and – as
Peter Stadlen put it, remembering one of the many coded phrases of
the time – 'became a U-boat'. Webern was then only restrained from
continuing to visit his friend of more than thirty years by Polnauer's
insistence that the risk to them both was too great.

By November 1940 Webern had completed another new work, an
elegantly written and beautifully constructed set of Variations for
Orchestra. As the spring of 1941 grew into summer he began to
compose what was to become the fourth movement of his Second
Cantata for soprano and bass soloists, chorus and orchestra, once
again to texts by Hildegard Jone. In December 1941 Japan attacked
the American naval base at Pearl Harbor in Hawaii, bringing the
hitherto neutral USA into the war against Japan's fellow Axis powers,
Germany and Italy. Webern must have realized that this meant the
end of any direct contact with Schoenberg and other colleagues in
America. Nevertheless he wrote to Hueber:

I perceived Japan's entry into the war as a fundamental, decisive turn
for the better*! A mighty event! ... For who knows what will yet come*
forth from these people! I must say that this thought fills me with a quite

*special confidence. For as I imagine them – the Japanese people – they
appear to me as a* completely healthy race*! Through and through! Does
not something new arise from that direction? Out of an* undamaged,
age-old soil*! I can only perceive it* that way*!*

It was America's entry into the war, however, combined with
Germany's ill-judged invasion of the Soviet Union in June 1941,
which was eventually to seal the fate of the Third Reich. But even at
the height of German and Japanese military success, Webern took
care to rein in his pro-Axis views where appropriate. When Luigi
Dallapiccola – married to a Jewess, and with deeply held anti-Fascist
political beliefs – met Webern in Vienna in March 1942, he described
the occasion in his diary.

> *I am happy because this evening, at the house of my friend [Alfred]
> Schlee [the director of Universal Edition], I had the good fortune to shake
> hands with Anton Webern. A mystic, a little man who speaks with some
> traces of an Austrian dialect; gentle, but capable of outbursts of anger;
> friendly to the point of treating me as his equal (he speaks of 'our common
> responsibilities') … The conversation turns to the war … It is easy for
> us to understand each other. On which side of the barricade we are,
> is written on our foreheads. We speak in dismayed tones of the fall
> of Singapore …*

The capture of Singapore, and with it the surrender of some
130,000 British and Commonwealth troops, had been the Imperial
Japanese Army's greatest single triumph of the Pacific War.

Along with his work on the Second Cantata, Webern's day-to-day
life centred on the happiness he drew from his domestic surroundings. He now had three grandchildren – Amalie's son, and Christine's
two daughters – on whom he doted. His own son Peter, too, had in
April 1941 married Hermine Schubert, the daughter of a carpenter in
the nearby village of Perchtoldsdorf. Missing his regular climbs in the
high mountains – now effectively prevented by wartime conditions –
and the sight of the high alpine flowers, Webern planted a small
garden in the yard behind Im Auholz 8 and tended it devotedly. In
February 1943 he managed to obtain a visa to travel to Winterthur
in Switzerland for the première, on 3 March, of his Variations for

Orchestra, conducted by Hermann Scherchen. It was the last time he was to hear any of his own music publicly performed.

The massive defeat of the German army at Stalingrad in February 1943, and with it the surrender of some 330,000 troops, marked a turning point in the war. Webern's son Peter, having earlier been discharged from the army on health grounds, was one of thousands of reservists who were now called up; he was assigned to occupied Yugoslavia where underground partisan activity, spurred on by the recent Russian victory, had become a serious problem for the German

German army graves on the Russian front, 1942

occupying forces. Webern's mood of militaristic optimism began rapidly to evaporate as he worried about his son, and about what now might lie in store for the Third Reich. 'When will it ever be *different?* [May] mankind [be] delivered from these dangers!' he wrote to Hueber in October. With the Allied invasion of Italy making steady progress, Vienna was now within range of enemy aircraft, and bombs began to fall on the city for the first time. 'To have to let such *horrible* things happen with *small children* holding your hand!' wrote Webern to Hildegard Jone. In the same letter he informed her that he was working on the sixth movement so far of the new Cantata.

His sixtieth birthday on 3 December 1943 was celebrated quietly in Vienna with a few friends. The occasion could not be marked by the local performance of any of his officially 'Jewish and Bolshevist' music; however Willi Reich, who was now living in Switzerland, had organized an all-Webern concert in Basel which took place two days later and included the belated première of the Three Songs Op. 23. Webern meanwhile had begun to compose a seventh movement for his Second Cantata. Then in January 1944 he suddenly realized that with some strategic re-ordering of the movements already written, the work was in fact complete. Writing excitedly to Hildegard Jone, he compared its final six-movement form with that of the Catholic mass: Kyrie, Gloria, Credo, Sanctus, Benedictus and Agnus Dei.

Indeed the Cantata's structural connection with one of the classic forms of Renaissance and Baroque choral music is strikingly close in some places (if less clear in others). The spiritual parallel, too, is unmistakable. The Second Cantata is Webern's most comprehensive and developed masterpiece in its wonderfully mature harvesting of a lifetime's creativity. It is also the work over which the spirit of the Netherlands masters hovers most closely – not so much the shade of Heinrich Isaac, perhaps, as that of Josquin des Près, whose music so winsomely combines technical intricacy with lightness of touch and a classically masterful sense of 'work-in-play'. It is fitting that the last piece of music that Webern is known to have completed was the Cantata's eventual third movement. '… It will be a very animated piece,' he had written to Hildegard Jone in October. 'Yet not so much something *excited* as (to express myself in Goethe's spirit) "*representing something excited*" – or so I hope at least.' This music's fierce brilliance of sonority – it is scored for solo soprano, three-part women's chorus, and orchestra – and its incisive, rhythmically bounding canonic writing together strike a note of ringing, even defiant affirmation. The Expressionist introspection of an earlier Webernian sound-world has long since been left distantly behind. At the summit of his life's work Webern was here composing music in which, down to the fibre of its being, everything is positive.

Early in 1944 he started on a new composition, which he conceived at first as a Second Concerto in three movements. Work on it soon had to be interrupted, as he wrote to the Humpliks in April:

> *I've been called up: air-raid protection police … So I am* 'embarracked', not allowed to live at home *and hence snatched utterly away from my work!!! … My post is* Mödling, *the secondary school is my billet, i.e.,* my barracks! *And in uniform of course. Endless grind from 6am to 5pm. Duties: roughly those of a* mason: *carrying sand and so on … I am tired, spent!*

Until his discharge from this dispiriting genre of active duty on 1 June, his main consolation was that Christine and Benno Mattel lived two doors away. Webern wrote to the Humpliks that he could talk to the children, who now included his third granddaughter, over the neighbouring fence. His depression at the increasingly frequent Allied bombing was then deepened by the decision of his daughter Maria – who had married Fred Halbich, a doctor, the previous year and now had a baby son, born in February – to move for the time being with Christine and her children to the village of Mittersill in the Salzburg Alps, where Maria's father-in-law owned a house. Progress on the new Concerto nonetheless continued, and took an unexpected turn. On 27 June Webern wrote to Hildegard Jone that the project had developed into a vocal work, and quoted for her the musical sketch for a setting of one of her poems beginning:

> *Das Sonnenlicht spricht:*
> *Aufgeht der Vorhang der Nacht! Durch Licht wird die Herrlichkeit*
> *sichtbar,*
> *sichtbar die Säulen des Seins: Sehet, die Farben stehn auf!*

(The sunlight speaks:
Up goes the curtain of the night! Through light the splendour becomes
visible,
and visible become the pillars of existence: Look, the colours are
emerging!)

It is possible that Webern took the sketches for what might have become a Third Cantata for soloists, chorus and orchestra with him when a month later, desperate to escape the air-raids for a while, he and Wilhelmine went to join Maria and Christine for a three-week stay in Mittersill.

Webern already knew the village – situated on the Salzach river some sixty kilometres southwest of Salzburg – and its mountain-ringed surrounding scenery; the highest neighbouring peak is the Grossvenediger, which he had climbed nine years before. 'It is wonderfully peaceful here!' he wrote to the Humpliks. '… We have a clear view over the valley to ice-covered peaks. Generally we spend most of the day with the children and the flock of grandchildren – all of whom are fit and looking extremely well.' The happiness of the interlude was darkened by the news that a bomb had damaged the Humpliks' studio in Vienna (it was later completely destroyed). 'The children all around us are so *calming*, so *elevating*!' wrote Webern to Hildegard Jone at the end of a sympathetic letter announcing his and Wilhelmine's imminent return. 'God help us! We want never to see anything but happiness before our eyes.'

From October onwards Webern travelled from Maria Enzersdorf into Vienna every weekday to work at the offices of Universal Edition, a necessary condition to avoid being drafted into a labour force. His daughter Amalie had had a second son, who to Webern's pleasure was born on 13 September, Schoenberg's seventieth birthday. He conveyed a message of greetings to the master through Willi Reich in Switzerland. There was little else to raise his and his compatriots' spirits as the bombs fell and the news from both fronts, where the Wehrmacht was being relentlessly thrown back by the Allied armies, became increasingly grim. 'The necessary concentration for composing is hardly possible any more,' he wrote to a former Singverein chorus member in November. During the winter's growing military chaos as the Red Army rampaged across eastern Europe

Following page, Russian troops fighting in Vienna, April 1945: their advance prompted the Webern family exodus to Mittersill.

towards Vienna, Peter von Webern was transferred from one post to another. On the evening of 10 February, in transit once again to Yugoslavia, he called in on his parents with his wife Hermine for a few hours before returning to his troop train. Four days later an Allied plane machine-gunned the train while it was standing outside a tunnel between Marburg (Maribor) and Agram. Peter was hit by a bullet and died that evening in a hospital train outside Marburg. The news did not reach Hermine until 3 March; she and her sister broke the news to her distraught parents-in-law that afternoon.

As the Red Army fought its way ever closer to Vienna, the air-raids by day and by night became virtually constant. Webern and Wilhelmine, who like everyone else must have heard stories of the Russian soldiers' justified reputation for looting and rape, were eventually granted the necessary pass to allow them to leave the city. Each carrying as much as they could in a rucksack, they set out before dawn on 31 March and walked about thirty kilometres westwards as far as the village of Neulengbach, on the railway line to Salzburg. (Wilhelmine could have been evacuated by bus with the city's other women and children, but refused to leave her husband.) The couple caught a train to Zell am See where, while waiting on the platform on 2 April for a connection to Mittersill, they quite by chance met Amalie Waller and her two little sons, who had been evacuated as far as Innsbruck; Amalie too had decided to try to join her sisters in Mittersill. The little group then made its way to the Halbichs' house where they were reunited with Maria, Christine and their children. After five days of savage fighting Vienna fell to the Russians on 13 April. Gunter Waller and Benno Mattel managed to make their separate ways to Mittersill, swelling the numbers crowded into the Halbich house to seventeen. Soon afterwards the Allied forces advancing from the west – first the French, then the Americans – occupied the village. Hitler committed suicide in his Berlin bunker on 30 April; the Third Reich surrendered unconditionally on 8 May.

The occupying Americans did their best help the refugees and local population crowded into Mittersill, but food and fuel were wretchedly short. Webern fell seriously ill with dysentery, gradually recovering in June despite the lack of medicine. By then Hermine von Webern had managed to make her way to Im Auholz 8; finding its contents ransacked by Russian soldiers who had been billeted there,

Allied bombing inflicted
heavy damage on Vienna:
above, the Albertina, 1945.

she set about salvaging what she could. News of this only reached
Webern when Gunter Waller, having successfully made the
hazardous journey to Vienna and back across the border between
the Russian and American occupation zones, was also able to
inform his father-in-law that he had been elected president of the
ISCM's reorganized Austrian section, which had already given its
first concert.

Slowly the advent of peacetime conditions and the beauty of the
countryside and the mountains around the upper Salzach valley
brought Webern a measure of serenity. 'Naturally there is only little,
very little of everything!' he wrote to Hermine, while sitting with
Wilhelmine beside the lake at Zell am See on 30 August. 'But one
can get that little! ... And how do *you* manage to get *through these
horrors*? We speak about it every day and imagine that at least your
garden provides some sustenance! ... *I creep about with difficulty!*
Thank God, though, it gets better every day. And Mother, although
very emaciated, is again quite well, the courageous, good, tireless one!
... Embracing you fondly, dear child, Your old father.' By now he

Mittersill as it looks today:
left, viewed from the south
towards the Hohe Tauern;
above, the village church;
right, Am Markt 101 outside
which Webern was shot on
15 September 1945

had heard that he was to be offered both a professorship to teach composition at the State Academy, and a permanent conducting post with the newly established Radio Vienna.

Sitting one day with Wilhelmine on a bench behind Mittersill's church, with the mountains surrounding the village like a crown, he said: 'I would like to be buried here some day.'

On the evening of 15 September Webern and Wilhelmine arrived for supper at Am Markt 101, the house on the outskirts of the village where Benno Mattel had found accommodation for himself and his family. Webern was keenly looking forward to smoking his first cigar in months – a small part of the proceeds of Benno's by now thriving black-market operation. After a cheerful family meal two Americans expected by Benno arrived to transact, as he thought, some lucrative pre-arranged business. In fact they were working undercover, with orders to fake the transaction, assemble enough evidence and arrest him.

Webern, Wilhelmine and Christine went next door to the room where the children were sleeping. After a while Webern could not resist sampling his cigar before he and Wilhelmine had to return to the Halbichs' house in time for the curfew.

At her suggestion, not wanting to disturb the children with the smell of cigar smoke, he stepped into the darkness just outside the house. The two Americans, who in the past hour had been treated by Mattel to three drinks each, drew their revolvers and placed Mattel under arrest; one of them, a cook named Raymond Bell, then rushed out of the house to fetch help. Stumbling into Webern in the darkness, he fired three shots and then ran off towards the village. Saying 'I've been shot' Webern staggered back into the house. As Wilhelmine and Christine laid him on a mattress he said quietly: 'It's over.' ('Es ist aus.') By the time that medical help arrived, he was dead.

His body was removed to the local military hospital; Benno and Christine were taken into custody, and Wilhelmine was left to spend the night alone with the children. Amalie Waller, woken by neighbours at four the next morning, found her father's body lying on the floor of a chapel which was being used as a morgue. During the military investigation that followed, Raymond Bell claimed that he had shot Webern in self-defence. Confronted with this, Wilhelmine

Opposite, Webern's grave in Mittersill as it now looks

replied: 'My husband was convalescent and weighed only about 50 kilos; he was about 160cms tall. According to my belief, it would be against his nature to attack anybody, especially a soldier.'

Martin Heiman, a German-born soldier summoned to the house by Bell immediately after the shooting, acted as interpreter throughout the investigation. He later commented:

> *I ... do not know what the investigation report stated about Mr A von Webern's role – apart from the testimony of his wife. But to the best of my knowledge not the slightest proof existed that he attacked the cook, apart from the testimony of the cook, who was about two heads taller than Mr A von Webern. I did not speak to a single officer familiar with the case who believed Mr von Webern was guilty of anything in this connection. Certainly in my opinion he was a completely innocent bystander.*

Webern was buried on the morning of 21 September in the cemetery of the village church in Mittersill.

Postscript

As the autumn of 1945 tilted towards winter, the people of Austria –
among them the surviving members of Webern's family – set about
the long process of rebuilding their lives and that of their bombed,
occupied, and war-shattered country.

When Amalie and Gunter Waller returned to Vienna in the early
autumn of 1945, Wilhelmine decided to stay on in Mittersill to
help her two other daughters look after their temporarily fatherless
families. Fred Halbich, Maria's husband, had been captured in
Yugoslavia; he was not to be repatriated until 1948, when he was to
see for the first time his and Maria's second child, a daughter born in
October 1945. Christine Mattel, who had been arrested on the night
of Webern's death as a possible accomplice in her husband's black-
marketeering, was released two days later. Benno Mattel was jailed for
a year; after his release he left for Italy, where Christine and the
children joined him in 1948. The family subsequently emigrated to
Argentina, one of several South American countries that were the
favoured destinations of German and Austrian ex-Nazis.

Throughout this period Hermine von Webern, Peter's widow,
continued to rescue Webern's belongings bit by bit from the wrecked
house in Maria Enzersdorf. Wilhelmine visited her former home a
few times – once taking some items from Webern's little alpine
garden back with her to plant on his grave in Mittersill – before the
gulf between past happiness and present grief became too great for
her. Refusing to set eyes on the house any more, she made the
occasional visit with Amalie to Hermine's home in Perchtoldsdorf to
sift through her late husband's possessions, once arranging for the sale
of some of these to help make ends meet. Otherwise she stayed in
Mittersill, from where she tried to generate interest in performances
of Webern's music. Asked to attend the première of the First Cantata
at the BBC in London in July 1946, she wrote to Hermine: 'How
painful it was for me that I could not be there. But I would not have
received a travel permit and would have had neither the money nor

the clothes for it.' True to form, a few performances of Webern's music did materialize abroad, but not in Vienna.

In August 1949 Wilhelmine moved to a single room on the upper floor of Am Markt 101, the house where Webern had died four years previously. She herself died there on 29 December, and was buried beside her husband. The final sadness of her life was that she did not live to witness the growing interest in her husband's music from the early 1950s onwards. Raymond Bell, who had returned home to America, never overcame his remorse at having caused Webern's death, and died of alcoholism in September 1955.

Austria, too, had by now embarked on the first stages of a new life which many had not lived to see. (Of the 220,000 Jews still in Austria in 1938, only about 5,000 remained by 1946. Josef Polnauer was among those who survived.) After the war Vienna, like the rest of the country, had been divided into four zones administered by America, Britain, France, and by the Soviet Union, which had occupied the eastern region around the capital. The constitution of 1920 and the country's status as an independent democratic republic were restored, and a national election was held in November 1945. The Austrian Communist Party's minuscule share of the vote showed clearly the political direction in which the Austrian people wished their post-war future to develop.

The Western powers, at last abandoning (at American prompting) their punitive and ultimately disastrous between-the-wars policy towards Austria, correctly and far-sightedly estimated that both their own interests and those of Austria herself would best be served by providing aid to help the country feed itself in the short term, and then to reconstruct its economy in the years ahead. Eventually the Soviet Union formed the Warsaw Pact for the mutual defence of its own borders and those of the other eastern European states now in the Soviet bloc. Assessing that Austria was no longer strategically essential to its interests, the Soviet Union agreed to withdraw its occupying forces from the country by the end of 1955. A state treaty, painstakingly negotiated with the Soviet Union and the Western powers, established Austria's permanent military neutrality; it also safeguarded the rights of Croatian and Slovenian minorities living within the country's borders. At last the Second Austrian

Republic was free to determine its own path towards post-war economic prosperity.

It has since done so with a success that is all the more striking when considered against the dreadful background of the inter-war years. National and racial tensions built up over centuries do not, of course, disappear in a generation. Whereas modern Germany has made genuine strides towards coming to terms with its immediate past – particularly its anti-Semitic past – it is perhaps fair to say that Austria's progress in this respect remains more ambiguous. For instance when German and Slovene dual-language signs were put up in 205 Carinthian towns and villages in 1972, they were torn down by some of the local German-speaking population. The situation only eased when, five years later, the national government decided that such signs should only be raised where more than a quarter of the community was not German-speaking. (Schwabegg's Slovenian name, as indicated on up-to-date maps, is Zvabek.) In a small way the resolution of this issue symbolizes one of the dominant features of post-war Austrian life: an often uneasy, but reasonably resilient instinct for political and social consensus.

The progress of Webern's music in the post-war world, meanwhile, has been rather more erratic than that of Austria herself.

In the late 1940s a resurgent avant garde of composers, looking to purge the culturally compromised inheritance of the recent past, set about forging a totally new musical language. A brave new world demands a figure who can be seen to combine the roles of idol and standard-bearer. Much as Schoenberg had acquired this status in the eyes of the young lions of Webern's generation in turn-of-the-century Vienna, so Webern himself now became the approved progenitor of the new post-war species of serial and post-serial composition – a cause vociferously espoused by the two most spectacular talents of the day, the French composer Pierre Boulez and his German contemporary, Karlheinz Stockhausen. Other major figures of the new generation who were influenced to varying degrees by Webern's 'pioneering' example were Jean Barraqué of France; Luigi Nono and Bruno Maderna of Italy; and in America, Milton Babbitt. (Any specifically Webernian influence on the music of the equally prominent György Ligeti, Luciano Berio and Hans Werner Henze is much harder to discern. And the musical creations of a whole army of Webern-influenced nonentities and fashion-followers have since deservedly sunk without trace.)

For these individuals and their associates at the conservatoires, colleges, summer schools, contemporary-music festivals and electronic studios of Europe and America during the 1950s, Webern also had the advantage of being dead. This meant that he was not in a position to hose down some of his posthumous adherents' more preposterous claims on his behalf; and so the newly proclaimed gospel of Webern as the father of 'the new music' – unsullied by anything as impure as a connection with the music of the past (e.g., that of the supposedly backward-looking Schoenberg) – was able to take root. There were other reasons for this entrenched misconception. Several of Webern's works were not published until the late 1950s and early 1960s, while several of his early, late-Romantic ones were presumed lost and were not re-discovered until 1965. The few works that were widely performed before then were mostly Webern's later instrumental pieces, particularly the Symphony and the Piano Variations. And given the avant-garde climate of the times, those performances were not noted for their emphasis on post-Mahlerian expressivity.

In 1959 Universal Edition published a performing edition of the Piano Variations annotated by Peter Stadlen, who had premièred the work in 1937. The music's basic notation is here enhanced by a remarkable array of additional indications relating to phrasing, articulation, dynamics and expression; suggestions made to Stadlen by Webern are printed in red, with further ideas of Stadlen's own added in green. The question therefore arises as to why, since this kind of expressive intensity was what Webern wanted when his music was performed, he nonetheless kept its notation pared down to less than the minimum markings that would clearly show this – a tragic situation, in Stadlen's view, since this same notational austerity would appear to license the desiccated brittleness which disfigured so many Webern performances in the immediate post-war years (and which sometimes still does). Perhaps because Webern himself either conducted or played in many of the performances of his music that took place during his lifetime, or was present at many of the rest to work with the artists involved, he did not fully realize the need for more detailed indications on which singers and players could draw in his absence. No doubt he would also have pointed out that his notation is in itself no sparer than Mozart's or Beethoven's, and that no sane performer accordingly assumes that *this* music requires depersonalized interpretation. But for many years, when it came to performing Webern, a dispiriting species of metronomic soullessness was the order of the day.

All this meant that Webern now came to be celebrated as the composer who had pointed the way to the future with a sequence of dry, spiky, hermetically sealed twelve-note works, each one constructed out of the musical equivalent of bits of aluminium scaffolding. Left-wing credentials were of course *de rigueur* in the immediate post-war age, and vague awareness of Webern's association with the Austrian Social Democratic Party ensured the final stages of his canonization. His later and highly inconvenient fixation with Nazism either remained unknown or was swept under the carpet. So was his equally inconvenient devotion to the music of the past in general, and to that of the supposed neo-Romantic reactionary Arnold Schoenberg in particular (to say nothing of the fact that the bulk of Webern's own music is of course vocal, not abstractly instrumental).

Schoenberg died in 1951, never having returned to Europe. The following year the 27-year-old Pierre Boulez wrote a polemically brilliant aesthetic obituary entitled 'Schoenberg is dead', in which Young Boulez Rampant relegated what he saw as Schoenberg's outdated practice of 'verifying serial technique by means of old forms' to the rubbish-heap of musical history. Had Webern lived, it is interesting to reflect on how he would have responded to this document. Very possibly a more recent generation of composition students would still be picking little pieces of Pierre Boulez off the wall of a rehearsal studio somewhere in Paris or Darmstadt. On the other hand Webern would surely have been thrilled to find his own music receiving the kind of widespread attention which until the 1950s it had been denied, even if he would also have insisted, fiercely, on widening the narrow artistic perspective within which that attention was focused.

When that same narrowness of perspective eventually helped to reverse the post-war ascendancy of serialism, Webern's achievement at first seemed to have been brought down with it. His music of course sounds almost entirely unlike Boulez's or Stockhausen's – much of which tends towards large-scale design and furious complexity in the very way that Webern's, on the whole, does not – but this did nothing to prevent its temporary eclipse due to guilt by association. Fortunately, however, the musical world has moved on from being browbeaten into the belief that the Boulezian genre of 'total serialism' – extending the principle of serial note-ordering to the areas of rhythm, dynamics, instrumentation and even to overall structure – was the only artistically valid path for a modern composer.

In the same way, Webern's music has now at last begun to make slow but genuine progress of its own, by being truthfully presented for what it is. The advent of a generation of singers able to cope idiomatically with its exacting vocal demands has helped. So has its suitability for recording and broadcasting, where those features which make it difficult to programme in most orchestral concerts – brevity, atmospheric spareness, and a preference for chamber-orchestra rather than symphonic forces – become real advantages. (Webern once remarked that he preferred to conduct in a broadcasting studio rather than in the concert-hall.) And it is a pleasing irony that Pierre Boulez, as an international conductor of great influence, has in recent decades probably done more than anyone else to present an accurate and broad-based overview of Webern's achievement – and indeed of Schoenberg's – to a non-specialist audience.

Genuine examples of Webern's influence on the work of other composers will always be rare: his music's style is too close to its idiosyncratic Austrian roots to be imitated other than superficially, and besides, the artistic standard that he set is simply too severe. It takes a great composer to engage in close and exact dialogue with the work of another and so to come up with masterpieces which, while bearing the imprint of the experience, are also unmistakably his or her own. Fortunately there is one great composer who has achieved precisely that.

Igor Stravinsky was a late convert to the splendours of the German tradition; until the 1950s, his affinity had been with the cultures of his native Russia and of his adopted France, with a nod to Italy. Stravinsky's sequence of late serial works which culminated in the *Requiem Canticles* of 1966 – his last major creation, and one of his supreme achïevements – remains the outstanding response so far by another composer to the unprecedented fusion of concentration and expressive power in Webern's later music. Somewhere within Stravinsky's quite different musical syntax – ritualistic, non-developmental, concerned with the rotation of self-contained musical cells rather than with a Webernian instinct for lyrical engagement – are the clues to the creative alchemy which brought this series of masterworks into being.

Considered more broadly, the most striking feature common to both composers is their understanding of the heart of the sonic phenomenon which we call music. The *Requiem Canticles* and Webern's First Cantata each draw on a conceptual apparatus both powerful and profound; but neither work is concept-*ridden*. The music speaks as sound. It is no coincidence that the least polemical, most perceptive, and most moving of all tributes to Webern has been penned not by a self-styled younger successor, but by the then 73-year-old Stravinsky, in an issue of the modern music periodical *Die Reihe* commemorating the tenth anniversary of Webern's death in 1955.

The 15th of September 1945, the day of Anton Webern's death, should be a day of mourning for any receptive musician.

We must hail not only this great composer but also a real hero. Doomed to a total failure in a deaf world of ignorance and indifference he inexorably kept on cutting out his diamonds, his dazzling diamonds, the mines of which he had such a perfect knowledge.

Classified List of Works

The catalogue that follows does not claim to be complete, for the simple reason that this is not literally possible in Webern's case. To include only those works for which Webern provided opus numbers would be unsatisfactory, since this would mean omitting many items which posterity can reasonably regard as 'essential Webern' (whatever he himself may have felt); and logically the orchestral arrangement of Bach's Ricercar from *A Musical Offering* would also have to be excluded, although Webern evidently considered to it be as important as any of his 'own' works. On the other hand if works without opus numbers are indeed to feature, then a judgement has to be made as to which ones to select.

This list therefore includes, along with Webern's works with opus numbers, many others that his heirs, archivists, and/or publishers have considered as meriting posthumous public exposure. Virtually all of those listed here have been published; absolutely all have been performed at least once, and are therefore liable to feature in concerts, on records or in broadcasts. No unperformed work or fragment has been included, although it is possible that such works may be performed and/or published in some form in the future. Webern would often abandon a sketch after writing down only a few bars of music, but other unfinished sketches or drafts are extensive enough for convincing performing versions at least notionally to be made. Also, given that many of Webern's possessions were lost in the chaos of occupied Vienna at the end of the Second World War, other unknown works may yet come to light besides those that have already been rediscovered. The reader in search of further information, especially regarding Webern's arrangements of his own and others' music and the numerous

surviving sketches and drafts of unfinished works, is referred to the meticulously detailed work-list in Hans Moldenhauer's *Anton von Webern: A Chronicle of his Life and Work* (see Further Reading).

Dates indicate the year when the actual musical composition of each work was finished; the instrumentation of those involving orchestra sometimes took a little longer. Also following Dr Moldenhauer's method, an asterisk is used to indicate works not collected or entitled as such by Webern, but which have since been performed and/or published in this form.

Webern's radical concept of what constituted an 'orchestra' makes it difficult accurately to classify his works in a catalogue of this kind in a way that always accords with his own choice of titles. The works here included as 'Orchestral' are those whose string parts require – as in the traditional sense of that classification – more than one instrument per section. Where Webern specifies solo strings only, these works – the Five Pieces for Orchestra Op. 10 and the Eight Orchestral Fragments – are included under 'Chamber/Instrumental'.

Choral with Instruments/Orchestra

(except where stated otherwise)

Entflieht auf leichten Kähnen, Op. 2, for unaccompanied chorus, text by Stefan George (1908). fp Fürstenfeld, Austria, 10 April 1927

Entflieht auf leichten Kähnen, Op. 2, with added instrumental accompaniment, text by Stefan George (1908, arranged 1914). fp Saarbrücken, Germany, 14 March 1969

Two Songs, Op. 19, texts by Johann Wolfgang von Goethe (1925–6). fp unknown (probably during recording by Columbia Masterworks, USA, 1957)

Das Augenlicht, Op. 26, text by Hildegard Jone (1935). fp London, 17 June 1938

First Cantata, Op. 29, text by Hildegard Jone (1938–9). fp London (BBC), 12 July 1946

Second Cantata, Op. 31, text by Hildegard Jone
(1941–3). fp Brussels, 23 June 1950

Vocal with Piano

Three Poems*, texts by Ferdinand Avenarius, Richard
Dehmel, Gustav Falke (1899–1903). fp Seattle, USA,
26 May 1962

Eight Early Songs*, texts by Richard Dehmel,
Johann Wolfgang von Goethe, Martin Greif, Wilhelm
Weigand, Friedrich Nietzsche, Matthias Claudius,
Detlev von Liliencron (1901–4). fp Seattle, USA,
27 May 1962

Three Songs*, texts by Ferdinand Avenarius (1903–4).
fp Seattle, 26 May 1962

Five Songs*, texts by Richard Dehmel (1906–8).
fp Seattle, 26 May 1962

Five Songs from *Der siebente Ring* by Stefan George,
Op. 3 (1908–9). fp Vienna, 6 June 1919 (individual
songs: Vienna, 8 February 1910)

Five Songs on poems of Stefan George, Op. 4
(1908–9, definitive version: 1920). fp Basel, Switzerland,
10 February 1940 (individual songs: Vienna,
8 February 1910)

Four Songs*, texts by Stefan George (1908–9).
fp Buffalo, USA, 29 October 1966

Four Songs, Op. 12, texts: anonymous, Li-Tai-Po
translated by Hans Bethge, August Strindberg, Johann
Wolfgang von Goethe (1915–17). fp unknown (entries
in Webern's diary indicate October 1926 for No. 4,
January 1927 for complete cycle)

Three Songs from *Viae inviae*, Op. 23, texts by
Hildegard Jone (1933–4). fp Basel, 5 December 1943

Three Songs, Op. 25, texts by Hildegard Jone (1934).
fp New York, 16 March 1952

Vocal with Instruments

Two Songs, Op. 8, texts by Rainer Maria Rilke (1910,
revised for publication, 1925). fp unknown (probably
during recording by Columbia Masterworks,
USA, 1957)

Schmerz, immer blick nach oben, text by Webern (1913).
fp New York, 11 April 1964 (see also Chamber Music/
Instrumental: Six Bagatelles for String Quartet)

Three Orchestral Songs, texts by Webern,
Stefan George (1913–14). fp Buffalo, 30 October 1966

Four Songs, Op. 13, texts by Karl Kraus, Wang-Seng-Yu
translated by Hans Bethge, Li-Tai-Po translated by
Hans Bethge, Georg Trakl (1914–18, No. 4 revised 1922).
fp Winterthur, Switzerland, 16 February 1928

Six Songs, Op. 14, texts by Georg Trakl (1917–21).
fp Donaueschingen, Germany, 20 July 1924

Five Sacred Songs, Op. 15, texts: anonymous,
Des Knaben Wunderhorn (1917–22). fp Vienna,
9 October 1924

Five Canons on Latin texts, Op. 16, texts:
anonymous/liturgical, *Des Knaben Wunderhorn*,
Psalm 50 (1923–4). fp New York, 8 May 1951

Three Traditional Rhymes, Op. 17, texts:
anonymous (1924–5). fp New York, 16 March 1952
(No. 2: New York, 8 May 1951)

Three Songs, Op. 18, texts: anonymous/liturgical,
Des Knaben Wunderhorn (1925). fp Los Angeles,
8 February 1954

Orchestral

Im Sommerwind, Idyll for large orchestra after a
poem by Bruno Wille (1904). fp Seattle, 25 May 1962

Passacaglia, Op. 1 (1908). fp Vienna, 4 November 1908

Five Movements for String Quartet, Op. 5, arranged for string orchestra (1909, arranged 1928, revised 1929). fp Philadelphia, 26 March 1930

Six Pieces for Large Orchestra, Op. 6, original version (1909). fp Vienna, 31 March 1913

Six Pieces for Orchestra, Op. 6, revised version for reduced forces (1909, arranged 1928). fp Berlin, 27 January 1929

Five Orchestral Pieces (1913). fp Cologne, 13 January 1969 (Nos. 1, 3, 5: Philadelphia, 14 April 1967)

Symphony, Op. 21 (1927–8). fp New York, 18 December 1929

Variations for Orchestra, Op. 30 (1940). fp Winterthur, Switzerland, 3 March 1943

Piano Solo

Satz für Klavier*, 'Piano Movement' (1906). fp Vienna, 2 December 1958

Sonatensatz (Rondo) für Klavier, 'Sonata Movement (Rondo) for Piano' (1906). fp Hanover, New Hampshire, USA, 2 August 1968

Kinderstück (1924). fp New York, 22 July 1966

Klavierstück*, 'Piano Piece' (1925). fp Vienna, 8 February 1963

Variations for Piano, Op. 27 (1935–6). fp Vienna, 26 October 1937

Chamber/Instrumental

Two Pieces for Violoncello and Piano* (1899). fp Cleveland, USA, 3 June 1970

Langsamer Satz, 'Slow Movement', for String Quartet (1905). fp Seattle, 27 May 1962

String Quartet (1905). fp Seattle, 26 May 1962

Rondo for String Quartet (1906). fp Hanover, New Hampshire, 1 August 1968

Piano Quintet (1907). fp Vienna, 7 November 1907

Five Movements for String Quartet, Op. 5 (1909). fp Vienna, 8 February 1910

Four Pieces for Violin and Piano, Op. 7 (1910, definitive version: 1914). fp Vienna, 24 April 1911

Six Bagatelles for String Quartet, Op. 9 (1911–13). fp Donaueschingen, 19 July 1924 (first performance of Nos. 1 and 6 in originally conceived Drei Stücke für Streichquartett, with Schmerz, immer blick nach oben [see above]: New York, 11 April 1964)

Five Pieces for Orchestra, Op. 10 (1911–13). fp Zürich, 22 June 1926

Eight Orchestral Fragments* (1911–13). fp Vienna, 16 March 1972

Sonata for Violoncello and Piano (1914). fp Cleveland, 3 June 1970

Three Little Pieces for Violoncello and Piano, Op. 11 (1914). fp Mainz, 2 December 1924

Trio Movement for Clarinet, Trumpet, and Violin* (1920). fp Baton Rouge, USA, 17 February 1978

Satz für Streichtrio*, 'Movement for String Trio' (1925). fp Vienna, 8 February 1963

String Trio Movement* (1925). fp Baton Rouge, 17 February 1978

String Trio, Op. 20 (1926–7). fp Vienna, 16 January 1928

String Trio Movement* (1927). fp Vienna,
16 March 1972

Quartet for Violin, Clarinet, Tenor Saxophone, and
Piano, Op. 22 (1928–30). fp Vienna, 13 April 1931

Concerto, Op. 24 (1931–4). fp Prague,
4 September 1935

String Quartet, Op. 28 (1936–8). fp Pittsfield,
Massachusetts, 22 September 1938

Arrangements

Franz Schubert: Five Songs (arranged for voice
and orchestra, 1903). fp Buffalo, 30 October 1966

Martin Plüddemann: *Siegfrieds Schwert*, ballad
for soprano or tenor voice and piano (arranged for voice
and orchestra, 1903). fp London, 3 December 1978

Arnold Schoenberg: *Gurrelieder*, Prelude and
Interludes (arranged for two pianos and four players,
i.e., double piano-duet, 1909–10). fp Vienna,
14 January 1910

Arnold Schoenberg: Five Pieces for Orchestra, Op. 15
(arranged for two pianos, 1912). fp unknown

Arnold Schoenberg: First Chamber Symphony, Op. 9
(arranged for chamber group, five players, 1922–3).
fp Barcelona, 29 April 1925

Franz Liszt: *Arbeiterchor* ('Workers' Chorus'), for bass
solo, male chorus and piano (arranged for bass solo,
mixed chorus and orchestra, 1924). fp Vienna,
13 March 1925

Franz Schubert: Six German Dances, D 820 (arranged
for orchestra, 1931). fp Berlin, 25 October 1931

Johann Sebastian Bach: *Fuga (Ricercata) a 6 voci* (Fugue
[Ricercar] in six-part counterpoint) from *Ein
musikalisches Opfer*, BWV 1079 (arranged for chamber
orchestra, 1934–5). fp London (BBC), 25 April 1935

Further Reading

The following list is restricted to material which is reader-friendly, and which should also be reasonably easy to locate in book shops, music shops, and music libraries.

Most of the numerous writings on Webern are in German; the majority of these have not been translated; and the bulk of Webern literature in all languages is analytical and/or polemical in intention and execution, an approach which is valid for the specialist but less useful for the general reader. The few analytical items listed here are included because they also contain material of more general interest, independently of the accompanying technical detail. This is particularly true of Hans Moldenhauer's *Anton von Webern: A Chronicle of his Life and Work* (see below), where detailed discussion of Webern's works is arranged in separate chapters, allowing the surrounding biographical narrative to read with maximum fluency. Those seeking information on specialist and/or foreign-language material, or on English-language writings published only in America, are referred to Zoltan Roman's bibliography in Moldenhauer's *Chronicle*, and also to the bibliography appended to Paul Griffiths's entry on Webern in *The New Grove Dictionary of Music and Musicians* (see below). The letters and other writings of Schoenberg, Berg, and Steuermann, while of background-illuminating interest in their own right, also regularly mention Webern, hence their inclusion here. Not included (apart from *The New Grove*) are entries in the numerous available surveys and dictionaries of twentieth-century music, where references to Webern are easy to locate.

Berg, A. *Letters to his Wife (Briefe an seine Frau,* Munich and Vienna, 1965), edited, translated and annotated by B. Grun (London, Faber & Faber, 1971)

Boulez, P. 'Anton Webern', *Stocktakings from an Apprenticeship (Relevés d'Apprenti,* Paris, 1966), collected and presented by P. Thévenin, translated by S. Walsh (Oxford, Clarendon Press, 1991)

Craft, R. 'Anton Webern', *The Score* No. 13, September 1955 (reprinted, with revisions, in booklet accompanying Columbia recordings of *Anton Webern —The Complete Music* [see Selective Discography])

Dallapiccola, L. 'Meeting with Anton Webern (Pages from a Diary)' (*Incontro con Anton Webern. Pagine di Diario,* 1945), translated by J. C. G. Waterhouse, *Tempo* No. 99, 1972

Foreman, L. 'Webern, the BBC and the Berg Violin Concerto', *Tempo* No. 178, September 1991

Gerhard, R. 'Some Lectures by Webern', *The Score* No. 28, January 1961

Griffiths, P. 'Anton Webern' in S. Sadie (ed.) *The New Grove Dictionary of Music and Musicians* (London, Macmillan, 1980); reprinted in *The Second Viennese School,* The New Grove Composer Biography Series (London, Macmillan, 1983)

Kolneder, W. *Anton Webern. An Introduction to his Works* (*Anton Webern. Einführung in Werk und Stil,* 1961), translated by H. Searle (London, Faber & Faber, 1968)

Krasner, L. 'About Webern as Conductor', in booklet accompanying the Continuum recording of Webern conducting Berg's Violin Concerto [see Selective Discography]

Mason, C. 'Webern's Later Chamber Music', *Music and Letters* No. 38, July 1957

Moldenhauer, H. with R. Moldenhauer *Anton von Webern: A Chronicle of his Life and Work* (New York, Alfred A. Knopf, and London, Victor Gollancz, 1978)

Moldenhauer, H. 'A Webern Pilgrimage', *Musical Times* No. 109, February 1968

The Death of Anton Webern: a drama in documents (New York, Philosophical Library, 1961)

'Webern, Anton von', *Encyclopaedia Britannica* (Macropaedia), fifteenth edition, 1974

Reich, W. 'Anton Webern: the man and his music', *Tempo* No. 14, March 1946

Schoenberg, A. *Letters* (*Briefe*, edited by E. Stein, 1958), translated by E. Wilkins and E. Kaiser (London, Faber & Faber, 1964)

Smalley, R. 'Webern's Sketches', *Tempo* Nos. 112/113/114, 1975

Stadlen, P. 'Serialism reconsidered', *The Score* No. 22, February 1958

'No real casualties?', *The Score* No. 24, November 1958

'The Webern Legend', *Musical Times* No. 101, 1960

Stein, E. 'Anton Webern', *Musical Times* No. 87, January 1946

Steuermann, E. *The Not Quite Innocent Bystander*, writings edited by C. Steuermann, D. Porter, and G. Schuller, translated by R. Cantwell and C. Messner (Lincoln and London, University of Nebraska Press, 1989)

Webern, A. *The Path to the New Music* (*Der Weg zur neuen Musik*, edited by W. Reich, 1960), translated by L. Black (original German edition Vienna, Universal Edition, 1960: English edition Pennsylvania, Theodore Presser Co., 1963, assigned 1975 to Universal Edition Publishing Inc., New Jersey)

Webern, A. *Letters to Hildegard Jone and Josef Humplik (Briefe an Hildegard Jone und Josef Humplik,* edited by J. Polnauer, 1959), translated by C. Cardew (original German edition Vienna, Universal Edition, 1959; English edition Pennsylvania, Theodore Presser Co., 1967)

'Letters of Webern and Schoenberg to Roberto Gerhard', *The Score* No. 24, November 1958

Wildgans, F. *Anton Webern* (*Anton Webern. Eine Studie*, 1967), translated by E. Temple Roberts and H. Searle (London, Calder & Boyars, 1966)

Various Authors *Die Reihe*, Vol. 2, 1955; special issue commemorating the tenth anniversary of Webern's death (Vienna, Universal Edition, 1955; 2nd revised edition, 1959)

Anton von Webern: Perspectives, anthology compiled by H. Moldenhauer, edited by D. Irvine (Seattle, University of Washington Press, 1966; London, Sidgwick and Jackson, 1967)

Selective Discography

Record libraries, and shops with good second-hand or deleted stocks, may well possess items other than those listed here. Some may even have the four-disc set of Webern's so-called Complete Works (i.e., apart from those without opus numbers) recorded under the general direction of Robert Craft in the 1950s. The reputation of this famous set – which for many years remained virtually the only Webern available on record – is such that it would be confusing to exclude it here; but for all its pioneering status, the fraught and brittle style of many of the performances did much to perpetuate a damagingly misleading impression of how Webern's music should sound. The major exception to this is Marni Nixon's singing of the voice-and-piano songs, which remains remarkable for its 'finer-than-violin' tuning (as Stravinsky put it) combined with beguiling spontaneity and musicianship. (It was Nixon, incidentally, who dubbed Natalie Wood's performance as Maria in the musical soundtrack of the film version of Leonard Bernstein's *West Side Story,* an accomplishment that the movie-smitten Webern would surely have appreciated.) Fortunately Pierre Boulez's 'complete' set on Sony Classical (again, complete regarding only those works with opus numbers) has substantially helped to set matters straight. The quality of the performances and of the recorded sound, though variable, is on the whole good; none of the performances could be described as an exercise in artistic distortion (unlike many in Craft's set); and the best – notably those of the Symphony, *Das Augenlicht* and the Second Cantata – are superlatively fine. (Boulez uses the original version of the Six Pieces for Orchestra Op. 6 rather than Webern's later revision, an important detail not mentioned in Sony Classical's sparse documentation.) The spontaneous intensity of Webern's conducting at its best, too, comes across vividly in the recordings of his arrangement of Schubert's German

Dances in Sony Classical's set, and of Berg's Violin Concerto on Continuum.

Among the other CDs, the Netherlands Ballet Orchestra's lovely playing of *Im Sommerwind* (on Koch-Schwann) can be warmly recommended; so can the London Symphony Orchestra's atmospheric way with the Five Pieces Op. 10 under Antal Dorati (Mercury), and the expressive expertise of Dorothy Dorow and the Netherlands Chamber Ensemble in their collection of Webern's songs with instrumental accompaniment (Koch-Schwann). The Berlin Philharmonic Orchestra's performances with Karajan on Deutsche Grammophon, though undeniably masterly, should nonetheless be approached with caution: their plush-velvet sumptuousness says more about the artistic priorities of Herbert von Karajan than about those of Anton von Webern.

Collections

Complete Works, Opp. 1–31
*Five Movements, Op. 5 (*version for string orchestra*)*
Bach arr. Webern: Fuga (Ricercata) from
     'A Musical Offering'
Various solo artists, Juilliard String Quartet, John Aldis Choir, London Symphony Orchestra conducted by Pierre Boulez
Schubert arr. Webern: Six German Dances
Frankfurt Radio Orchestra conducted by Anton Webern (29 December 1932)
Sony Classical S3K 45845 (3 CDs)

Complete Works, Opp. 1–31
Bach arr. Webern: Fuga (Ricercata) from
     'A Musical Offering'
Various artists, various ensembles conducted by Robert Craft
Columbia Masterworks K4L-232 (4 LPs); issued in Europe on Philips (4 LPs)

Piano Quintet
Entflieht auf leichten Kähnen (original
    unaccompanied version)
Two Songs (Rainer Maria Rilke)
Five Pieces for Orchestra, Op. 10
Four Songs, Op. 13
Six Songs (Georg Trakl)
Five Sacred Songs
Five Canons
Three Traditional Rhymes
Three Songs, Op. 18
Two Songs (Johann Wolfgang von Goethe), Op. 19
Quartet, Op. 22
Concerto
Françoise Pollet (soprano), Christiane Oelze (soprano),
Pierre-Laurent Aimard (piano), BBC Singers, Ensemble
InterContemporain conducted by
Pierre Boulez
DEUTSCHE GRAMMOPHON 437 786-2

Orchestral

Im Sommerwind
Passacaglia
Six Pieces for Orchestra, Op. 6 (revised version)
Five Pieces for Orchestra, Op. 10
Five Pieces for Orchestra (1913)
*Bach arr. Webern: Fuga (Ricercata) from
    'A Musical Offering'*
Variations for Orchestra, Op. 30
Netherlands Ballet Orchestra conducted by
Roelof van Driesten
KOCH-SCHWANN 3-1069-2

Passacaglia
Five Movements, Op. 5 (version for string orchestra)
Six Pieces for Orchestra, Op. 6
Symphony
Berlin Philharmonic Orchestra conducted by
Herbert von Karajan
DEUTSCHE GRAMMOPHON 423 254-2

Five Pieces for Orchestra, Op. 10
London Symphony Orchestra conducted by
Antal Dorati; with works by Schoenberg and Berg
MERCURY 432 006-2

Passacaglia
Five Movements, Op. 5 (version for string orchestra)
Six Pieces for Orchestra, Op. 6
Symphony
Berlin Philharmonic Orchestra conducted by
Herbert von Karajan; with works by Schoenberg
and Berg
DEUTSCHE GRAMMOPHON 427 424-2 (3 CDs)

Six Pieces for Orchestra, Op. 6
Berlin Philharmonic Orchestra conducted by
James Levine; with works by Schoenberg and Berg
DEUTSCHE GRAMMOPHON 419 781-2

Vocal/Choral

Three Poems (1899–1903)
Three Songs of Ferdinand Avenarius
Five Songs of Richard Dehmel
*Five Songs from 'Der siebente Ring' by
    Stefan George, Op. 3*
Five Songs on poems of Stefan George, Op. 4
Four Songs (Stefan George)
Four Songs, Op. 12
Three Songs from 'Viae inviae' (Hildegard Jone), Op. 23
Three Songs (Hildegard Jone), Op. 25
Dorothy Dorow (soprano), Rudolf Jansen (piano)
ETCETERA KTC 2008

Songs for voice and piano (selection)
Dietrich Fischer-Dieskau (baritone), Aribert
Reimann (piano); with Schoenberg's *Gurrelieder*
and songs by Schoenberg and Berg
DEUTSCHE GRAMMOPHON 431 744-2

Entflieht auf leichten Kähnen (original unaccompanied
version/version with instrumental accompaniment)
Two Songs (Rainer Maria Rilke)
*Drei Stücke für Streichquartett (includes 'Schmerz,
immer blick nach oben')*
Three Songs (1913/14)
Four Songs, Op. 13
Six Songs (Georg Trakl)
Five Sacred Songs
Five Canons
Three Traditional Rhymes
Three Songs, Op. 18
Two Songs (Johann Wolfgang von Goethe), Op. 19
Dorothy Dorow (soprano), Netherlands Chamber
Choir, Schoenberg Ensemble conducted by Reinbert
de Leeuw
KOCH-SCHWANN CD 314 005 H1

Chamber/Piano

String Quartet (1905)
Five Movements, Op. 5
Six Bagatelles
String Quartet, Op. 28
LaSalle Quartet; with complete string quartets by
Schoenberg and Berg
DEUTSCHE GRAMMOPHON 419 994-2 (4 CDs)

String Quartet (1905)
Langsamer Satz (1905)
Rondo (1906)
Five Movements, Op. 5
Six Bagatelles
String Quartet, Op. 28
Artis Quartet; with music by Michael Gielen
SONY CLASSICAL SK48059

Langsamer Satz (1905)
String Quartet (1905)
Five Movements, Op. 5
Six Bagatelles
String Quartet, Op. 28
Quartetto Italiano
PHILIPS CLASSICS 420 796-2

Variations for Piano, Op. 27
Maurizio Pollini (piano); with piano works by
Boulez, Prokofiev, and Stravinsky
DEUTSCHE GRAMMOPHON 419 202-2

Rondo for String Quartet (1906)
Piano Quintet (1907)
Satz für Streichtrio (1925)
String Trio
LaSalle Quartet, Stefan Litwin (piano); with music
by Schoenberg
DEUTSCHE GRAMMOPHON 437 036-2

Webern as Conductor

Alban Berg: Violin Concerto
Louis Krasner (violin), BBC Symphony Orchestra
conducted by Anton Webern (1 May 1936); with
Berg's *Lyric Suite* for string quartet
CONTINUUM SBT 1004

Index

Page numbers in italics refer to
picture captions.

Photographic
Acknowledgements

Archiv für Kunst und Geschichte,
    London: 58, 96, 112–13, 174,
    175t+b, 179c+b, 185, 192, 197,
    199, 206, 210–11
Archiv für Kunst und Geschichte,
    Berlin: 181
Arnold Schoenberg Institute
    Archives, University of
    Southern California: 123,
    128r, 141
Associated Press, London: 179t,
    189b
Austrian National Tourist Office,
    London: 9, 167, 171
British Library, London: 91
Generaldirektion für die Post- und
    Telegraphenverwaltung,
    Vienna: 35L

Hayes, Malcolm: 22–3, 70l, 72,
    109, 147, 162–3, 187, 214,
    215l, 217
Historisches Museum der Stadt
    Wien: 30r, 62l, 121t, 130
Hulton-Deutsch Collection,
    London: 26l, 40–1, 54–5, 59l,
    76–77, 84, 88–9, 93, 98–9,
    124–5, 152–3, 189t
Kärntner Landesarchiv, Klagenfurt:
    131l
Lebrecht Collection: 118
Mansell Collection, London: 30l,
    35r
Österreichisches National-
    bibliothek, Vienna: 26r, 43, 81,
    104–5, 121b, 131t, 159, 213
Paul Sacher Foundation, Basel:
    cover, 2, 13, 16lr, 19, 20, 31, 45,
    62r, 110, 115, 120l+r, 129r, 148
Range Pictures Ltd, London: 47,
    51, 128l, 176
Richard-Wagner-Museum,
    Bayreuth: 33
Segantini Museum, St Moritz: 69
Steirisches Tourismus GmbH,
    Graz: 134–5
Universal Edition, Vienna: 156, 165,
    178, 202, 215r